hamlyn
QuickCook

hamlyn

QuickCook
Gluten-Free
Meals

Recipes by Joy Skipper

Every dish, three ways—you choose!
30 minutes | 20 minutes | 10 minutes

An Hachette UK Company
www.hachette.co.uk

First published in Great Britain in 2014 by Hamlyn,
a division of Octopus Publishing Group Ltd
Endeavour House, 189 Shaftesbury Avenue
London WC2H 8JY
www.octopusbooks.co.uk

Distributed in the U.S. by Hachette Book Group USA,
237 Park Avenue, New York NY10017 USA
www.octopusbooksusa.com

Distributed in Canada by Canadian Manda Group,
165 Dufferin Street, Toronto, Ontario, Canada M6K 3H6

Recipes by Joy Skipper
Copyright © Octopus Publishing Group Ltd 2014

ISBN 978-0-600-62706-7

A CIP catalogue record for this book is available from the British Library

Printed and bound in China

10 9 8 7 6 5 4 3 2 1

Ovens should be preheated to the specified temperature. If using a convection oven,
follow the manufacturer's instructions for adjusting the time and temperature.
Broilers should also be preheated.

This book includes dishes made with nuts and nut derivatives. It is advisable for
those with known allergic reactions to nuts and nut derivatives and those who may
be potentially vulnerable to these allergies, such as pregnant and nursing mothers,
people with weakened immune systems, the elderly, babies, and children, to avoid
dishes made with nuts and nut oils.

It is also prudent to check the labels of prepared ingredients for the possible inclusion
of nut derivatives.

The U.S. Food and Drug Administration advises that eggs should not be consumed
raw. This book contains some dishes made with raw or lightly cooked eggs. It is
prudent for more vulnerable people, such as pregnant and nursing mothers, people
with weakened immune systems, the elderly, babies, and young children, to avoid
uncooked or lightly cooked dishes made with eggs.

Contents

Introduction

30 20 10—Quick, Quicker, Quickest

This book offers a new and flexible approach to planning meal for busy cooks, letting you choose the recipe option that best fits the time you have available. Inside you will find 360 dishes that will inspire and motivate you to get cooking every day of the year. All the recipes take a maximum of 30 minutes to cook. Some take as little as 20 minutes and, amazingly, many take only 10 minutes. With a little preparation, you can easily try out one new recipe from this book each night and slowly you will be able to build a wide and exciting portfolio of recipes to suit your needs.

How Does it Work?

Every recipe in the QuickCook series can be cooked one of three ways: a 30-minute version, a 20-minute version, or a superquick-and-easy 10-minute version. At the beginning of each chapter, you'll find recipes listed by time. Choose a dish based on how much time you have and turn to that page.

You'll find the main recipe in the middle of the page accompanied by a beautiful photograph, as well as two time-variation recipes below.

If you enjoy your chosen dish, why not go back and cook the other time-variation options at a later date? So, if you liked the 20-minute Mint-Crusted Lamb Cutlets with Mashed Peas, but only have 10 minutes to spare this time around, you'll find a way to cook it using quick ingredients or clever shortcuts.

If you love the ingredients and flavors of the 10-minute Egg-Filled Mushrooms on Toast, why not try something more substantial, such as the 20-minute Poached-Egg Topped Mushroom Soup, or be inspired to make a more elaborate version, such as Mushroom and Egg Pizzas? Alternatively, browse through all 360 delicious recipes, find something that catches your eye, then cook the version that fits your time frame.

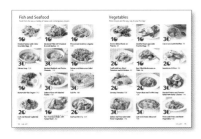

Or, for easy inspiration, turn to the photo gallery on pages 12–19 to get an instant overview by themes, such as Fish and Seafood or Vegetarian Dishes.

QuickCook Online

To make life easier, you can use the special code on each recipe page to e-mail yourself a recipe card for printing, or e-mail a text-only shopping list to your phone. Go to www.hamlynquickcook.com and enter the recipe code at the bottom of each page.

GLU-SNAX-MUX

QuickCook Gluten-Free Meals

Gluten is a protein composite found in wheat, rye, and barley that has the ability to "hold" foods together and gives dough made from these grains elasticity. Eating a gluten-free diet means avoiding these grains as well as other foods that contain added gluten.

Some people react to eating foods that contain gluten, especially those people who have celiac disease, where the gluten causes inflammation in the small intestine. Celiac disease is a medically diagnosed autoimmune condition in which gluten causes an allergic reaction in the digestive tract, possibly leading to malabsorption of certain nutrients and a range of symptoms, including fatigue, weight loss, and skin conditions. It has been estimated that as many as one percent of the population cannot tolerate gluten, and the rise in celiac disease has created a huge demand for gluten-free recipes.

However, in recent years eating a gluten-free diet has also become something of a trend, despite the fact that there is no evidence to suggest that eliminating gluten from your diet has any significant benefits for the general population. The only way to be sure of which products or foods affect you adversely is by avoiding them for a few weeks and then reintroducing them one at a time while monitoring your symptoms. If you are on a gluten-free diet to test if your symptoms will improve without gluten, be aware that it may take a while: 3–4 weeks would be a reasonable time to allow.

Approaching the Gluten-Free Diet

When switching to a gluten-free diet, it can initially seem as if there is nothing that you can safely eat. A gluten-free diet rules out all ordinary breads, pasta, and many convenience foods, such as gravies, soup,s and sauces, because gluten is also used as an additive in the manufacture of a wide number of foods—for example, as a flavoring or thickening agent in ice cream or ketchup.

According to the Codex Standard for food for special dietary use for persons intolerant to gluten (CODEX STAN11-1979), most, but not all, gluten-sensitive individuals can tolerate oats. Other research suggests that cross-contamination in milling facilities may be to blame for symptoms, or when oats are grown in rotation with wheat. Reading food labels is vital when approaching the gluten-free diet, because there is gluten hidden in many foods, such as soy sauce (use tamari as an alternative), snack foods, meatballs, salad dressing, Worcestershire sauce, dry-roasted nuts, spice mixes, processed meats, and even beer (the gluten is in the barley).

In other countries, foods can be labeled as "gluten-free" if they contain no more than 20 parts per million gluten. This labeling do not currently occur in the United States, although the Food and Drug Administration has proposed a similar type of labeling regulation in 2007.

Gluten-Free Ingredients

In the past few years the number of gluten-free foods available has increased greatly, with most major supermarkets stocking a range of gluten-free foods to choose from. The following are suggestions for gluten-free alternatives:

corn (cornstarch, cornflakes, corn pasta)
buckwheat (blinis, udon noodles)
gluten-free oats (oatmeal, oat cakes)
rice (brown, basmati, wild, noodles, crackers, etc.)
millet (flakes, grains, flour, bread)
quinoa (grains, flakes, flour)
potatoes (flour)
kelp noodles
sago and tapioca
legumes (chickpea flour or pasta, soy flour or bread)
nuts (coconut, chestnut, almonds flours)
flax

People who follow a gluten-free diet may have low levels of certain vitamins and other nutrients in their diet, because many grains are enriched with vitamins. Gluten-free food isn't necessarily healthy, however, especially if people are following a gluten-free diet just to be trendy, or in an attempt to lose weight—there is the chance of missing important nutrients, such as iron, the B vitamins (needed for energy), and fiber (important for detoxification). The best sources of iron are meat, poultry, fish, beans, and leafy green vegetables, which are all gluten-free.

It may be advisable to visit a nutritionist for advice on how to increase foods that are abundant in these nutrients in your diet and to discuss supplementation if you want to make sure you are consuming a basic level of nutrients.

Making Your Meals Gluten-Free

Learning to cook gluten-free food is a challenge, but not an impossible one. Once you know which ingredients you are allowed to have and which you should avoid, adapting most recipes is simply a case of trial and error. One school of thought is that when cooking gluten-free food it's best to make only things that were never meant to contain gluten, for example cornmeal and orange cake, or ground almond chocolate cake, but with so many special ingredients now available, especially from online sources, most recipes can be adapted to be gluten-free.

Keeping your menu simple is obviously important to start with—go back to the basics to get a few staple recipes under your belt before you experiment with more complicated recipes. Fresh meat, fish, vegetables, and fruit are all gluten-free and can be used for a whole host of recipes. Fresh eggs, cheese, and other dairy products are also safe to use if additive-free (always read labels, because even store-bought grated cheese sometimes has wheat in it). To be sure there is no cross-contamination in your kitchen, always store your gluten-free foods separately, especially if there is more than one person doing the cooking.

Experiment with different gluten-free flours. There are plenty to choose from—rice flour, coconut flour, quinoa flour, almond flour, buckwheat flour—and they all have different textures and tastes, so it may take a while to get used to how they react in cooking and how they taste. You can also buy flour mixes that are gluten-free, and these are probably the best ones to start with.

As with all diets, being organized is the best way to be sure you will stick to the diet. Planning your weekly meals in advance, shopping with a list of foods you are allowed (and reading labels on the foods you buy), and cooking meals from scratch will all help to make life easier and ensure you are eating a balanced diet. This book includes recipes that will help you to keep to a gluten-free diet throughout the day—filling breakfasts, nutritious lunches, and tasty family meals—in addition to plenty of baked goods and sweet treats to help you realize that you are not missing out on anything at all.

Meaty Treats

Flavor-packed meals to please all meat lovers

Brunch Bacon Tortilla 56

Buttermilk Pancakes with Bacon and Syrup 58

Corned Beef Hash 90

Pea and Ham Soup 132

Butternut, Asparagus, and Prosciutto Salad 144

Beef Carpaccio and Bean Salad 150

Peppered Steak and Red Onion Salad 154

Roast Pork Chops with Apple and Celery Salad 164

Mint-Crusted Lamb Cutlets with Mashed Peas 194

Sausage and Onion with Mustard Mashed Potatoes 210

Quick Pancetta and Broccoli Pizza 212

Broiled Liver with Sage Lentils 214

Chicken and Duck

Nutricious and delicious poultry dishes for every occasion.

Chicken Salad Wraps 68

Duck and Lettuce Wraps 76

Chicken and Vegetable Satay 80

Chicken and Tarragon Pesto Penne 106

Chicken, Red Pepper, and Roasted Sweet Potato 112

Honey and Mustard Chicken Salad 152

Chicken and Cashew Nut Curry 166

Roasted Duck Breast with Plum Sauce 174

Creamy Herb-Stuffed Chicken Breast 192

Mediterranean Olive Chicken 198

Thai Chicken Meatballs with Spaghetti 206

Chicken en Papillote with Mashed Celeriac 216

Fish and Seafood

Fresh from the sea, a medley of classic and contemporary recipes.

Smoked Salmon with Chive Scrambled Egg 28

Mackerel Pâté with Steamed Broccoli Quinoa 92

Broccoli and Anchovy Linguine 108

Salmon Soup 124

Smoked Haddock and Potato Chowder 130

Salmon and Watercress Salad 146

Homemade Fish Sticks 162

Salmon Stew with Mashed Potatoes 170

Fish Casserole 186

Crab and Mussel Tagliatelle 190

Pan-Fried Red Snapper with Mashed Fennel 202

Seafood Stir-Fry 208

Vegetarian Meals

These recipes are the easy way to your five day!

Boston Baked Beans on Polenta 38

Grilled Asparagus with Poached Eggs 70

Carrot and Lentil Muffins 78

Fusilli with Sun-Dried Tomatoes and Artichokes 82

Egg-Filled Mushrooms on Toast 86

Corn Fritters 94

Savory Pancakes 100

Italian Bean and Truffle Soup 120

Roasted Potato and Tomato Salad with Goat Cheese 136

Quinoa and Feta Salad with Roasted Vegetables 156

Macaroni and Cheese with Leeks 168

Pasta with Pesto and Roasted Vegetables 196

Spicy Dishes

Add a hint of heat with these sweet and savory recipes.

Kedgeree 44

Shrimp with Spicy Dip 74

Spicy Turkey Burgers with Red Pepper Salsa 84

Spicy Sweet Potato and Red Pepper Soup 128

Sesame Seared Tuna with Spicy Coriander Salad 148

Mackerel Curry 178

Spaghetti Arrabiata with Chile and Shrimp 184

Spicy Lamb Stew 200

Stir-Fried Mixed Vegetables with Cashew Nuts 218

Baked Apples with Spiced Fruit 236

Spicy Grilled Pineapple 244

Chile Hot Chocolate 248

Fruity Favorites

Mouth-watering recipes that are packed with seasonal fruit favorites.

Blueberry Pancakes 26

Sweet French Toast with Berries and Orange Yogurt 32

Breakfast Banana Split 50

Creamy Mango Smoothie 54

Grapefruit and Sea Bass Tacos 98

Quick Watercress, Beet, and Orange Salad 138

Sweet Orange Crepes 224

Coconut and Raspberry Muffins 228

Fruit-Stuffed Crepes 250

Date and Amaretti Tiramisu 254

Banana-Caramel Pie 262

Lemon and Turkish Delight Syllabub 274

Summer Selection

Let the sun shine with these light and refreshing summer options.

Honey Granola 36

Roasted Peppers 64

Salmon Blinis 66

Broiled Sardines with Pan-Fried Lemon Potatoes 88

Barbecued Vegetable Kebabs with Herb Dipping Sauce 96

Salmon Ceviche 102

Chilled Avocado Soup 122

Lima Bean, Tomato, and Feta Salad 134

Quick Roasted Pepper Pizza 172

Amaretti-Stuffed Peaches 240

Strawberries & Meringue with Ginger 256

Lemon and Raspberry Cheesecake Tartlets 278

Winter Classics

Banish cold and gray with hearty winter recipes.

Berry and Coconut Oatmeal 34

Cheese and Herb Biscuits 40

Butternut Squash and Chickpea Soup with Hash Browns 118

Leek and Arugula Soup 126

Tagliatelle with Dolcelatte and Walnut Sauce 176

Spiced Lamb Casserole 180

Mushroom Risotto 182

Ratatouille Pizza 204

Caramelized Pears with Salted Caramel Sauce 230

Rhubarb Whip 232

Blueberry and Date Mousse 238

Blackberry and Apple Crisps 252

QuickCook

Breakfast and Brunch

Recipes listed by cooking time

30

20

10

1⏲ Muesli

Serves 4

2¼ cups rolled oats
⅓ cup dried cranberries
⅓ cup chopped dried apricots
⅓ cup chopped dates
½ cup chopped pecans
½ cup chopped Brazil nuts
3–4 tablespoons seeds
   (sunflower, pumpkin,
   and sesame)

To serve

milk
plain yogurt
fresh fruit

- Mix together all the dry ingredients.

- Divide among 4 bowls and serve with milk, yogurt, and fresh fruit.

2⏲ Muesli Bars

In a saucepan, melt 1¾ sticks unsalted butter with 1 cup firmly packed dark brown sugar and 2 teaspoons honey. Stir in 6 cups muesli, 2 tablespoons chopped pecans, and ¾ cup chopped dried apricots. Spoon into a 9 inch square pan and press down. Cook in a preheated oven, at 350°F, for 15 minutes. When cooked, cut into bars and let cool in the pan.

3⏲ Swiss-Style Muesli

Make the muesli as above, then put into a bowl and stir in 2 grated apples (with skin) and pour over enough milk, orange juice, or apple juice to just cover. Let soak for 20 minutes. Serve with plain yogurt and fresh fruit.

 # Blueberry Pancakes

Serves 4

1 cup gluten-free flour blend

2 teaspoons gluten-free baking powder

1 egg

⅔ cup soy milk

2 tablespoons unsalted butter, melted

⅔ cup blueberries

1 tablespoon olive oil

To serve

crème fraîche or plain yogurt

maple syrup

- In a large bowl, mix together the flour and baking powder.
- Whisk together the egg and milk and whisk into the flour until smooth.
- Whisk in the melted butter, then stir in ½ cup of the blueberries.
- Heat the oil in a skillet over medium heat, then spoon tablespoons of the batter into the skillet. Cook for 3–4 minutes, until golden underneath, then flip over and cook for another 2–3 minutes. Repeat with the remaining batter.
- Serve with the remaining blueberries, a dollop of crème fraîche or yogurt, and a drizzle of maple syrup.

Blueberry Smoothie

Put 3 cups apple juice, 1⅔ cups plain yogurt, 3 chopped bananas, and 3½ cups blueberries into a bender and blend until smooth, adding a little milk if too thick. Pour into 4 glasses to serve.

Blueberry Muffins

Sift together 2 cups gluten-free flour blend, 1 tablespoon gluten-free baking powder, and ½ teaspoon baking soda. Stir in ⅓ cup sugar. Mix together 4 tablespoons unsalted butter, melted, 2 eggs, and ⅔ cup milk, then stir into the flour, adding 1 cup blueberries when nearly combined. Line a 12-section muffin pan with paper liners and spoon in the batter. Bake in a preheated oven, at 400°F, for 15 minutes, until golden and slightly risen. Remove from the pan and cool on a rack.

Smoked Salmon with Chive Scrambled Eggs

Serves 4

8 eggs
2 tablespoons fromage blanc
  or heavy cream
1 tablespoon chopped chives
4 oz smoked salmon,
  cut into strips
salt and black pepper
4 slices gluten-free bread,
  toasted and buttered, to serve

- Using a handheld wire whisk, whisk the eggs and fromage blanc or heavy cream together with some salt and black pepper.

- Heat a saucepan over medium heat and pour in the egg mixture. Cook for a minute, and then using a spatula, gently push the egg around to help it all cook.

- When the egg looks like creamy curds, stir in the chives and smoked salmon and serve immediately on the toast, if using.

 Smoked Salmon Bagels with Poached Eggs and Deviled Tomatoes Toast both sides of 4 halved gluten-free bagels for 2–3 minutes. Spread each bagel with ¼ cup cream cheese and top with 2 oz sliced smoked salmon. Mix 1 tablespoon olive oil with ½ teaspoon ground cumin and ½ teaspoon curry powder. Cut 4 tomatoes in half and brush the cut halves with the spicy oil. Cook under a medium broiler for 5–6 minutes. Poach 4 eggs in a skillet of simmering water for 4-5 minutes. Serve the bagels topped with a poached egg and a sprinkling of chopped chives, with the tomatoes on the side.

Smoked Salmon Frittata Thickly slice 1 lb new potatoes and cook in boiling water for 8–10 minutes. Drain. Lightly beat 8 extra-large eggs, then stir in 8 oz strips of smoked salmon, 2 tablespoons chopped dill, ⅔ cup small green peas, and the potatoes. Season. Heat 2 tablespoons olive oil in a skillet with an ovenproof handle. Pour in the egg mixture and cook over low heat for 10–15 minutes, until the egg is starting to set. Place under a preheated medium broiler and cook for 3–4 minutes, or until the egg is set and the top is golden. Turn out onto a board and cut into wedges to serve.

30 Cocoa, Orange, and Pecan Oat Bars

Serves 4

oil, for greasing
½ cup coconut oil
¼ cup molasses
2 tablespoons packed
  dark brown sugar
1 tablespoon agave syrup
2¾ cups rolled oats
½ cup coarsely chopped pecans
½ cup cocoa nibs or gluten-free
  semisweet chocolate chips
finely grated zest of 1 orange

- Grease a 7 inch square baking pan.

- In a large saucepan, melt together the coconut oil, molasses, sugar, and agave syrup until the sugar has dissolved.

- Stir in the remaining ingredients and mix well.

- Pour into the prepared pan and level the top.

- Bake in a preheated oven, at 350°F, for 18–20 minutes, then remove from the oven and cut into 12 squares. Let cool in the pan.

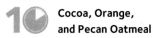

Cocoa, Orange, and Pecan Oatmeal

Put 2½ cups rolled oats into a saucepan with 2½ cups milk and 2½ cups water. Bring to a boil, then simmer for 8–9 minutes, stirring from time to time so the oats don't stick to the bottom of the pan. Stir in the finely grated zest of 1 orange, then serve sprinkled with 1 tablespoon cocoa nibs or gluten-free semisweet chocolate chips and 1 tablespoon chopped pecans and drizzled with 1 tablespoon honey.

Cocoa, Orange, and Pecan Muesli

Lightly toast ½ cup pecans and ½ cup Brazil nuts for 2–3 minutes, then coarsely chop. Mix with 2¼ cups rolled oats, ⅓ cup chopped dried apricots, ½ cup chopped prunes, ⅓ cup chopped dates, ½ cup cocoa nibs or semisweet chocolate chips, and 2–3 tablespoons pumpkin seeds and sesame seeds. Pour into a bowl, cover with orange juice, and let stand for 10 minutes. Serve with plain yogurt and fresh fruit.

# Sweet French Toast with Berries and Orange Yogurt

Serves 4

⅔ cup blueberries

⅔ cup hulled and quartered strawberries

2 oranges

1⅔ cups Greek yogurt

2 eggs, beaten

¼ cup superfine or granulated sugar

2 tablespoons sesame seeds

pinch of ground cinnamon

2 tablespoons unsalted butter

4 slices of gluten-free bread

- Put the blueberries and strawberries into a bowl. Grate the zest of the oranges and reserve, then segment the oranges, catching all the juice. Add the orange segments and the juice to the berries.

- Stir the orange zest into the yogurt and chill.

- Whisk together the eggs, sugar, sesame seeds, and ground cinnamon.

- Melt the butter in a skillet over medium heat. Dip the slices of bread into the egg mixture, place in the pan, and cook for 2–3 minutes on each side, until golden.

- Serve each slice of French toast topped with fruit and a dollop of the yogurt, with the juices poured over the top.

 Warm Berry Compote and Yogurt Put 1 cup raspberries, ¾ cup blueberries, and 1⅓ cups hulled and halved strawberries into a small saucepan with 2 tablespoons honey and heat through for 6–7 minutes, stirring from time to time. Divide 2 cups Greek yogurt among 4 small bowls or glasses and pour the warm compote over it. Serve immediately.

 Dried Fruit Compote with Lemon Yogurt Grate the zest of 1 lemon and stir into 1⅔ cups Greek yogurt with 1 tablespoon lemon curd. Chill. Put 1 cup dried fruits, such as apricots, prunes, and cranberries, into a saucepan with 2 pitted and chopped plums. Add ½ teaspoon ground cinnamon and 1¼ cups orange juice and simmer for 15–18 minutes over low heat. Let cool for 5 minutes, then serve with the lemon yogurt.

10 Berry and Coconut Oatmeal

Serves 4

2½ cups rolled oats

2½ cups milk

¼ cup plain yogurt

1½ cups fresh berries, such as raspberries, blueberries, and hulled halved or quartered strawberries

3 tablespoons dry shredded coconut, plus extra to sprinkle

¼ cup honey

- Put the oats into a saucepan with the milk and 2½ cups water. Bring to a boil, then simmer for 8 minutes, until thick and creamy, stirring often.

- Pour into 4 warm bowls and stir in a swirl of the yogurt.

- Top with the berries and a drizzle of honey, then sprinkle with dry shredded coconut.

20 Berry and Coconut Quinoa

Put 1 cup quinoa into a saucepan with 1¼ cups milk, ½ cup water, ¾ cup raspberries, and ¼ teaspoon ground cinnamon. Bring to a boil, then simmer for 12–15 minutes, until the liquid is absorbed and the quinoa is cooked. Serve topped with 2 chopped bananas and ⅔ cup blueberries, a sprinkling of dry shredded coconut, and a drizzle of honey.

30 Berry and Coconut Pancakes

Blend ¾ cup dry shredded coconut in a food processor for 2–3 minutes, then pour into a bowl and mix with ½ cup quinoa flour and 1 teaspoon gluten-free baking powder. Whisk in 1 egg, ⅔ cup coconut milk, and 3 tablespoons superfine or granulated sugar, then let the batter stand for 10 minutes. Stir in 1⅓ cups blueberries. Heat a skillet over medium heat and lightly grease with vegetable oil.

Pour tablespoons of the batter into the skillet and cook for 2–3 minutes, until set and golden underneath, then flip over and cook for another 1–2 minutes. Remove from the pan and keep warm while cooking the remaining pancakes. Serve the pancakes on warm plates, topped with a few more blueberries and a drizzle of honey.

3 Honey Granola

Serves 4

1 tablespoon honey
2 teaspoons maple syrup
1 tablespoon sunflower oil
1 tablespoon warm water
¼ cup firmly packed light
   brown sugar
1¼ cups steel-cut oats
½ cup whole almonds
¼ cup whole Brazil nuts, chopped
3 tablespoons dried cranberries
⅓ cup dry shredded coconut

To serve
plain yogurt
fresh berries

- Whisk together the honey, maple syrup, oil, measured water, and sugar.

- Stir in the remaining ingredients, except the cranberries and coconut, and mix well.

- Put the mixture onto a baking pan and spread evenly. Bake in a preheated oven, at 300°F, for 15 minutes, then add the cranberries and coconut and bake for another 10 minutes. Remove from the oven and pour onto a baking sheet to cool. Let cool completely. Store in an airtight container.

- Serve with plain yogurt and fresh berries.

 Cinnamon and Honey Oatmeal

In a small saucepan, mix 2¼ cups rolled oats with ½ teaspoon ground cinnamon and 3 cups water or milk (whichever you prefer). Cook over medium heat for 8–9 minutes, stirring occasionally, until the oatmeal thickens. Serve topped with chopped banana and a drizzle of honey.

 Honey-Drizzled Pancakes

Mix together 1 cup gluten-free flour blend and 1 teaspoon gluten-free baking powder. Whisk in 1 egg and ⅔ cup soy milk until you have a smooth batter. Whisk in 2 tablespoons butter, melted. Heat 1 tablespoon olive oil in a skillet over medium heat, then spoon tablespoons of the batter into the skillet and cook for 3–4 minutes, until golden underneath. Flip over and cook for another 2–3 minutes on the other side. Repeat with the remaining batter and serve warm, drizzled with honey.

10 Boston Baked Beans on Polenta

Serves 4

2 tablespoons olive oil

2 large onions, chopped

1 teaspoon medium curry powder

½ cup raisins

2 (15 oz) cans baked beans

⅓ cup mango chutney

4 tablespoons butter

4 slices of store-bought
   polenta log

½ cup slivered almonds

- Heat half the oil in a saucepan over medium heat, add the onions, and sauté for 2–3 minutes, until beginning to soften. Stir in the curry powder, raisins, baked beans, and mango chutney. Cook for 4–5 minutes, stirring occasionally.

- Meanwhile, heat the butter and remaining oil in a skillet over medium heat, add the polenta, and cook for 1–2 minutes on each side.

- Serve the beans spooned over a slice of polenta, sprinkled with the slivered almonds.

---

20 Deviled Tomatoes with Cheesy

Polenta Brush 4 slices of a store-bought polenta log with a little olive oil and cook under a preheated hot broiler for 5 minutes on one side. Turn over, sprinkle with ¾ cup shredded cheddar cheese and broil for 3–5 minutes. Place 12 halved tomatoes on a large piece of aluminum foil, cut side down, and broil for 3–4 minutes. Turn the tomatoes over. Mix 2 tablespoons olive oil with 2 crushed garlic cloves, 2 teaspoons dry mustard, 1 teaspoon curry powder, and 1 teaspoon ground cumin and spoon a little of the mixture over each tomato. Broil for another 3–4 minutes. Spread each slice of polenta with 1 tablespoon mango chutney and top with the deviled tomatoes to serve.

30 Cornmeal Breakfast Pizza

Bring 4 cups water to a boil in a saucepan, then slowly pour in 2 cups cornmeal or polenta, stirring constantly. Season with salt and black pepper and add 2 tablespoons chopped parsley. Cook for another 8–10 minutes, or according to package directions, until the mixture is thick. Pour half the mixture out onto a lightly oiled baking sheet and spread into a circle about ½ inch thick. Repeat with the rest of the mixture. Bake in a preheated oven, at 400°F, for 12 minutes. Meanwhile, cook 8 unsmoked bacon slices under a preheated hot broiler for 5–6 minutes, or until crisp, then coarsely break into small pieces. Top each cornmeal circles with 2–3 tablespoons tomato paste or tomato sauce and spread it to within ½ inch of the edge. Divide 8 sliced tomatoes, the bacon pieces, and ¾ cup shredded cheddar between the cormeal circles and bake for another 10–12 minutes, until the cheese is golden and bubbling. Serve hot, cut into wedges.

3 0 Cheese and Herb Biscuits

Serves 4

2¾ cups gluten-free flour blend
3½ teaspoons gluten-free
  baking powder
1 teaspoon dry mustard
pinch of cayenne pepper
5 tablespoons unsalted butter
1¾ cups shredded cheddar cheese
1 tablespoon chopped chives, or
  herb of your choice
2 extra-large eggs
⅓ cup buttermilk
butter, to serve

- Sift the flour, baking powder, dry mustard, and cayenne into a large bowl.

- Rub in the butter until the mixture resembles bread crumbs. Mix in 1½ cups of the shredded cheese and the herbs.

- Beat the eggs with the buttermilk and mix into the flour, making a soft dough; do not overwork the dough.

- Turn out onto a lightly floured work surface and roll out to a thickness of 1 inch. Stamp out 12 biscuits, using a 2 inch cutter, and place onto a baking sheet.

- Sprinkle the remaining cheese over the biscuits and bake in a preheated oven, at 425°F, for 15 minutes, until risen and golden.

- Serve the biscuits warm, with butter.

 Cheese and Herb Pitas

Toast 4 gluten-free pita breads under a preheated medium broiler for 2–3 minutes on each side. Sprinkle with 3½ cups shredded cheddar mixed with ¼ cup chopped chives and place under a preheated hot broiler for 2–3 minutes, until golden and bubbling.

 Cheese and Herb Muffins

Mix together ⅔ cup cornmeal, ¾ cup almond flour, ⅔ cup tapioca (cassava) flour, 1 tablespoon gluten-free baking powder, ¼ teaspoon paprika, ¾ cup shredded cheddar cheese, and 2 tablespoons chopped chives. Mix together ½ cup sunflower oil, 2 eggs, and 1 cup milk, then mix the liquid ingredients into the dry ingredients to make a batter. Line a 12-section muffin pan with paper liners and spoon the batter into them. Sprinkle each one with 2 teaspoons shredded cheddar and bake in a preheated oven, at 375°F, for 17–18 minutes, until golden.

20 Huevos Rancheros

Serves 4

2 tablespoons olive oil

1 large onion, diced

2 red bell peppers, seeded
and diced

2 garlic cloves, crushed

¾ teaspoon dried oregano

1 (14½ oz) can diced tomatoes

4 eggs

2 tablespoons crumbled
feta cheese

4 toasted gluten-free pita breads,
to serve

- Heat the oil in a skillet over medium heat, then add the onion, bell peppers, garlic, and oregano and cook for 5 minutes.

- Add the tomatoes and cook for another 5 minutes. Pour the tomato mixture into a shallow ovenproof dish and make 4 dips in the mixture.

- Crack the eggs into the dips, sprinkle with the feta, and cook under a preheated hot broiler for 3–4 minutes.

- Serve with toasted pita breads.

 Tomatoes, Cheese, and Egg on Toast Poach 4 eggs in a skillet of simmering water for 4–5 minutes. Meanwhile, toast 4 slices of gluten-free bread. Top each one with a sliced tomato and sprinkle with 1⅓ cups shredded cheddar cheese. Place under a preheated hot broiler for 2–3 minutes, or until golden and bubbling. Top each slice of toast with a poached egg to serve.

 Traditional Mexican Huevos Rancheros Cook 7 peeled and diced red-skinned or white round potatoes in boiling water for 3–4 minutes. Drain well. Heat 2 tablespoons olive oil in a skillet and add the potatoes. Cook for 5 minutes, until they are crisp and golden, then remove with a slotted spoon. Add 1 chopped onion, 2 chopped garlic cloves, and 1 seeded and diced red chile to the skillet and cook for 2–3 minutes, then add 2 seeded and sliced red bell peppers and 4 quartered tomatoes. Return the potatoes to the pan, season to taste, then pour into an ovenproof dish. Make 4 dips and crack an egg into each one. Bake in a preheated oven, at 400°F, for 15–18 minutes, until the eggs are just set. Sprinkle with 1 tablespoonful chopped parsley to serve.

3⦿ Kedgeree

Serves 4

1 lb smoked haddock, or other smoked fish, such as cod or mackerel, or fresh white fish, such as haddock, cod, or halibut

4 tablespoons butter

1 onion, chopped

¾ teaspoon curry powder

1 cup long-grain rice

4 eggs, hard-boiled, peeled and quartered

2 tablespoons chopped parsley

½ lemon

- Put the haddock into a saucepan and cover with 2½ cups cold water. Bring to a simmer, cover, and cook for 8–10 minutes.

- Drain the fish, reserve the liquid and keep the fish warm.

- Using the same pan, melt the butter, add the onion, and sauté for 1–2 minutes, until softened. Stir in the curry powder and then the rice.

- Pour in 2 cups of the reserved fish water, bring to a simmer, cover, and cook for 15 minutes, or according to the package directions, until the rice is tender and the water has been absorbed.

- Skin and flake the fish and stir it into the rice with the quartered eggs.

- Serve sprinkled with chopped parsley and a squeeze of lemon juice.

1⦿ Smoked Haddock Pâté

Poach 12 oz smoked haddock fillet or other smoked fish in a saucepan of simmering water for 5–6 minutes, drain, skin, and put into a blender. Add 2 teaspoons lemon juice, ¼ cup plain yogurt, a pinch of cayenne pepper, and a dash of Worcestershire sauce. Blend until smooth. Serve in individual ramekins with slices of toasted gluten-free bread.

Poached Smoked Haddock and Egg on Toast

Poach 4 (5 oz) smoked haddock fillets in 1¼ cups simmering milk for 5–6 minutes. Drain and place on a baking sheet. Poach 4 eggs in a skillet of simmering water for 4–5 minutes, then keep warm. Melt 2 tablespoons butter in a saucepan over medium heat and stir in ⅓ cup gluten-free flour blend. Cook for 1 minute, then slowly pour in ½ cup beer, stirring constantly. Stir in 1⅓ cups shredded cheddar cheese, 1 egg yolk, 1 tablespoon Worcestershire sauce, 1 teaspoon mustard, and a pinch of cayenne pepper. Cook, stirring constantly, until the cheese melts and the sauce is smooth. Spoon the cheese mixture over the fish and broil under a preheated hot broiler for 1–2 minutes, until lightly browned and bubbling. Top each fillet with a poached egg.

2⃝ Omelet Arnold Bennett

Serves 4

⅔ cup light cream

8 oz smoked haddock, or other smoked fish, such as cod or mackerel, or fresh white fish, such as haddock, cod, or halibut

4 eggs, separated, plus 2 egg whites

½ tablespoon butter

1 tablespoon shredded Gruyère cheese or Swiss cheese

black pepper

crisp green salad, to serve

- Put the cream and black pepper to taste in a medium skillet and add the smoked haddock skin side up. Bring to a simmer.

- Remove the fish with a slotted spoon and skin and flake it. Return the fish to the pan and stir into the cream.

- Whisk together the egg yolks in a bowl. In a separate, grease-free bowl, whisk the egg whites until stiff. Gently fold the egg yolks into the egg whites.

- Melt a little butter in each of 2 omelet pans or small skillets, then pour half the egg mixture into each. Move it around a little until it starts to cook.

- When the bottom of each omelet is cooked, pour the creamy haddock mixture over it and sprinkle with the shredded Gruyère. Place under a preheated hot broiler and broil for 2–3 minutes, until starting to turn golden.

- Halve the omelets and serve on 4 plates with a crisp green salad. If preferred, cook one omelet in a large skillet and cut into quarters before serving.

 Poached Egg-Topped Smoked Haddock Cook 4 (5 oz) fillets of smoked haddock or other smoked fish in 1¼ cups simmering milk for 5 minutes. Poach 4 eggs in a skillet of simmering water for 4–5 minutes. Toast 4 slices of gluten-free bread and spread each with 2 tablespoons butter and sprinkle with some chopped chives. Place the haddock on the toast and top with a poached egg. Sprinkle with pepper to serve.

 Smoked Haddock and Egg Risotto Melt 4 tablespoons butter in a saucepan over medium heat, add 1 thinly sliced leek, and cook for 1–2 minutes. Stir in 1½ cups risotto rice and cook, stirring constantly, for 2 minutes. Pour in 3 cups fish stock and 1 cup milk, bring to a boil, and then simmer for 5 minutes. Pour the rice mixture into a buttered ovenproof dish and top with 12 oz skinless smoked haddock or other smoked fish, cut into large chunks. Cover and bake in a preheated oven, at 400°F, for 15–18 minutes. Meanwhile, poach 4 eggs in a skillet of simmering water for 4–5 minutes and keep warm. Remove the risotto from the oven and stir in 2 tablespoons chopped chives. Divide among 4 shallow bowls and serve topped with a poached egg.

3 Potato and Brussels Sprout Cakes with Poached Eggs

Serves 4

8 red-skinned or white round
  potatoes, peeled and quartered
4 tablespoons unsalted butter
6 cups trimmed and halved
  Brussels sprouts
⅓ cup gluten-free flour blend
3–4 tablespoons olive oil
4 eggs
salt and black pepper
chopped chives, to serve

- Boil the potatoes for 12–15 minutes, until tender, then drain and mash with the butter.

- Meanwhile, cook the Brussels sprouts in boiling water for 3–4 minutes, until just tender. Drain and refresh under cold running water.

- Mix together the sprouts and potatoes and season with salt and black pepper. Shape the mixture into 8 round cakes and dust with the flour.

- Heat the oil in a skillet over medium heat and cook the cakes in 2 batches, for 2–3 minutes on each side, until golden.

- Meanwhile, poach the eggs in a skillet of simmering water for 4–5 minutes, depending on how you prefer your eggs.

- Divide the cakes among 4 plates, top each with a poached egg, and sprinkle with chopped chives to serve.

1 Mountain Eggs

Heat ¼ cup olive oil in a large skillet. Add 4 large peeled, cooked, and chopped potatoes to the pan and cook for 2 minutes. Stir in 1⅓ cups chopped smoked ham and make 4 dips in the mixture. Crack one egg into each dip and top each with ¼ cup shredded Emmental or Swiss cheese. Place under a preheated hot broiler for 2–3 minutes, until the eggs are set and the cheese is golden and bubbling.

2 Cheesy Potato and Cabbage

Cook 7 peeled and chopped red-skinned or white round potatoes in a large saucepan of boiling water for 6–8 minutes, then add ½ shredded savoy cabbage and cook for another 4 minutes, or until the potatoes are tender. Drain and coarsely crush with 4 tablespoons unsalted butter. Season with salt and black pepper. Heat 2 tablespoons olive oil in a skillet over medium heat, add the potato mixture, and cook for 6–7 minutes. Sprinkle with 1 cup shredded cheddar or American cheese and cook under a preheated hot broiler for 2 minutes, until bubbling and golden.

1⃝ Breakfast Banana Split

Serves 4

4 tablespoons unsalted butter

2 tablespoons honey

4 bananas, cut in half lengthwise

2 sweet, crisp apples, grated

1¼ cups Greek yogurt

finely grated zest of 1 orange

½ cup walnuts, toasted

2 tablespoons slivered almonds, toasted

2–3 tablespoons maple syrup

- Melt the butter in a skillet with the honey until it sizzles.
- Place the bananas in the skillet, cut side down, and cook for 3–4 minutes, until golden.
- Meanwhile, mix together the grated apple, yogurt, and orange zest.
- Spoon the bananas onto 4 warm plates and top with a large dollop of the yogurt mixture.
- Sprinkle with the nuts, then drizzle with the maple syrup and any juices from the pan to serve.

2⃝ Banana and Yogurt Scones

Sift 2 cups gluten-free flour blend into a bowl with 1 teaspoon gluten-free baking powder. Rub in 4 tablespoons unsalted butter until the mixture resembles fine bread crumbs. Stir in ¼ cup superfine or granulated sugar. Whisk together 1 egg and ⅔ cup milk and pour into the flour mixture. Bring the dough together. Using an ice cream scoop, scoop 10 mounds of the dough onto a baking sheet. Bake in a preheated oven, at 425°F, for 12–15 minutes, until risen and golden. Serve warm with plain yogurt and sliced bananas.

3⃝ Banana Buckwheat Pancakes

Put 1 cup buckwheat flour into a bowl and whisk in 3 egg yolks, 1 teaspoon honey, ¼ teaspoon gluten-free baking powder, and a pinch of ground cinnamon. Slowly whisk in ⅔ cup milk. In a grease-free bowl, whisk 3 egg whites until soft peaks form and fold into the batter. Heat 1 tablespoon olive oil in a skillet over medium heat, add a few tablespoonfuls of the batter and cook for 2–3 minutes on each side, until golden. Repeat with the remaining batter and keep warm. Meanwhile, in another skillet melt 4 tablespoons butter with 2 tablespoons honey, then stir in 3 sliced bananas and cook for 3–4 minutes, until golden. Spoon the honeyed bananas over the pancakes to serve.

GLU-BREA-NOT

3⊙ Potato Cakes with Cream Cheese and Smoked Salmon

Serves 4

2 potatoes, peeled and chopped
2 tablespoons unsalted butter
⅓ cup rice flour
pinch of salt
1 teaspoon gluten-free
baking powder
1 egg, beaten
2 tablespoons olive oil

To serve

1 cup cream cheese
10 oz smoked salmon
chopped chives

- Cook the potatoes in a saucepan of boiling water for 10–12 minutes, until tender. Drain and mash with the butter until light and fluffy.

- Sift in the flour, salt, and baking powder, then add the egg and mix into a dough.

- Turn out onto a lightly floured work surface and roll to a thickness of about ¼ inch. Cut into 8 wedges and prick all over with a fork.

- Heat the oil in a skillet over medium heat and cook the wedges for 4–5 minutes on each side, until golden.

- To serve, spread each wedge with a little cream cheese, top with smoked salmon, and sprinkle with chopped chives.

 Bagels with Cream Cheese and Smoked Salmon Slice 4 gluten-free bagels in half and toast for 2–3 minutes on each side. Spread each bagel with ¼ cup cream cheese with chives and top each with 2 oz smoked salmon. Squeeze the juice of 1 lemon over the bagels and sprinkle with black pepper to serve.

 Potato and Smoked Salmon Hash Cook 5 russet or Yukon gold potatoes, peeled and cut into cubes, in a saucepan of boiling water for 10–12 minutes, until tender. Meanwhile, place 12 oz salmon fillets under a preheated hot broiler and cook for 3–4 minutes on each side. Break the fish into large flakes.

Heat 1 tablespoon olive oil in a skillet over medium heat, add 1 chopped red onion and 1 seeded and chopped red bell pepper, and cook for 3–4 minutes. Drain the potatoes, add to the pan, and cook for another for 6–8 minutes, then stir in the flaked salmon. Season and serve.

1⏱ Creamy Mango Smoothie

Serves 4

4 ripe mangoes, peeled and pitted
¼ cup plain yogurt
1 banana, peeled and chopped
4 cups soy milk
honey, to sweeten (optional)
ice cubes, to serve

- Put all the ingredients except the honey and ice into a blender and blend until smooth.

- Taste for sweetness and add honey, if required, then blend again.

- Pour into 4 tall glasses and serve with ice cubes.

2⏱ Mango with Orange Dressing and Marmalade Yogurt

For the marmalade yogurt, stir 1 tablespoon chunky marmalade into ¼ cup Greek yogurt and chill. For the orange dressing, put ⅓ cup granulated sugar and 1 split vanilla bean in a saucepan over low heat and melt gently. Stir in the grated zest and juice of 4 oranges and 3 tablespoons packed light brown sugar and simmer for 8–9 minutes, until syrupy.

Meanwhile, peel 4 mangoes and slice off the cheeks. Heat a ridged grill pan until smoking hot. Dust the mango cheeks with 2–3 tablespoons confectioners' sugar and chargrill for 2–3 minutes on each side. Serve the mango with a dollop of marmalade yogurt and a drizzle of orange dressing.

3⏱ Marinated Mango Salad

In a bowl, toss together 4 peeled, pitted, and chopped mangoes, 2 segmented oranges, 1 cup blueberries, and 1 tablespoon shredded mint leaves. Mix together 1 tablespoon honey, the zest and juice of 2 limes, and ¼ teaspoon ground cinnamon. Pour the marinade over the mango salad and let marinate at room temperature for 25 minutes. Serve with crème fraîche or Greek yogurt.

30 Brunch Bacon Tortilla

Serves 4

2 tablespoons olive oil
4 unsmoked bacon slices
6 extra-large eggs
4 red-skinned or white round
  potatoes, peeled, cooked,
  and diced
8 cherry tomatoes, halved
1 tablespoon chopped parsley
⅔ cup shredded cheddar cheese
salt and black pepper

- Heat 1 tablespoon of the oil in a skillet over medium heat, add the bacon, and cook for 3–4 minutes. Remove with a slotted spoon.

- Beat the eggs in a large bowl with some salt and black pepper, then stir in the bacon, potatoes, tomatoes, and parsley.

- Heat the remaining oil in the skillet over high heat, pour in the egg mixture, and cook for 1–2 minutes, then turn down the temperature.

- Cook for 12–15 minutes, keeping an eye on the edges to make sure the tortilla is not getting too cooked underneath; the top will still be runny.

- Sprinkle with the shredded cheddar cheese and then place the pan under a preheated hot broiler and cook for 3–4 minutes, until golden and bubbling.

- To turn out, place a plate on top of the pan and turn upside down.

- Cut into wedges to serve. This can be eaten hot or cold.

 Crispy Bacon with Scrambled Eggs

Broil 4 unsmoked bacon slices for 6–8 minutes, until crisp, then break into pieces. Meanwhile, beat 6 eggs with ¼ cup milk and 2 tablespoons chopped chives. Melt a pat of butter in a saucepan, pour in the egg mixture, and cook, stirring, for 5–6 minutes, until nearly set. Spoon onto plates and sprinkle with the bacon bits.

 Bacon-Baked Eggs

Melt 4 tablespoons butter in a saucepan over medium heat, add 1 finely diced shallot and 4 unsmoked bacon slices, diced, and cook for 1–2 minutes. Add ¾ cup chopped white button mushrooms to the pan and cook for another 3–4 minutes. Stir in 1 teaspoon chopped chives, season with salt and black pepper, and divide the mushroom mixture among 4 lightly buttered ramekin dishes, making a dip in the center of each. Break an egg into each dish, top each egg with 1 tablespoon of light cream, and season. Stand the dishes in a roasting pan filled halfway with hot water and bake in a preheated oven, at 350°F, for 10–15 minutes, until the whites are just set and the yolks are still runny.

30 Buttermilk Pancakes with Bacon and Maple Syrup

Serves 4

1 egg, beaten
¾ cup buttermilk
2 tablespoons butter, melted
⅓ cup tapioca or rice flour
3 tablespoons fine cornmeal
1 teaspoon baking soda
1 tablespoon sunflower oil
8 unsmoked bacon slices
maple syrup, to serve

- Whisk together the egg, buttermilk, and melted butter. Sift in the flour, cornmeal, and baking soda and mix together gently; do not overmix.

- Heat the oil in a skillet over medium heat and pour in 3 large spoonfuls of the batter to make 3 pancakes. Cook for 2–3 minutes, until bubbles start to appear. Flip the pancakes over gently and cook for another 1–2 minutes. Remove from the pan and keep warm.

- Repeat with the remaining batter to make a total of 12 pancakes.

  Meanwhile, cook the bacon under a preheated hot broiler for 3–4 minutes on each side until crisp.

- Serve the pancakes in stacks of 3 topped with the bacon slices and drizzled with maple syrup.

 Bacon and Egg Club Sandwich

Toast 12 slices of gluten-free white bread for 2–3 minutes on each side. Meanwhile, broil 8 unsmoked bacon slices for 3–4 minutes on each side until crisp and fry 4 eggs to your liking. Spread 4 slices of toast with 2 tablespoons ketchup and top with the bacon. Cover with 4 more slices of toast and top these with 4 sliced tomatoes. Place the eggs on top of the tomatoes and top with the remaining slices of bread to make 4 sandwiches. Secure with toothpicks and slice in half to serve.

 Breakfast Bacon and Sausage Pitas

Cook 4 link sausages under a preheated hot broiler for 8–10 minutes, turning regularly. Toast 4 gluten-free pita breads for 2–3 minutes on each side. Broil 8 unsmoked bacon slices for 3–4 minutes on each side, until crisp. Spread each pita with ½ tablespoon ketchup, then top with the bacon, followed by the sausages, cut in half lengthwise. Fry 4 eggs to your liking and place on top of the sausages. Sprinkle with ½ cup shredded cheddar or American cheese and place under a hot broiler for 2–3 minutes, until the cheese is bubbling.

QuickCook

Snacks and Light Lunches

Recipes listed by cooking time

3○

2○

10

30 Roasted Peppers

Serves 4
(or 8 as an appetizer)

2 red bell peppers, halved
   and seeded
2 yellow bell peppers, halved
   and seeded
1 small red onion, cut into
   8 wedges
½ cup green bean pieces
1 zucchini, halved and sliced
3 cloves garlic, sliced
2 tablespoons extra virgin olive oil
1 teaspoon cumin seeds
salt and black pepper
feta or goat cheese, to serve

- Place the bell pepper halves in a roasting pan and divide the other vegetables and the garlic among them.

- Sprinkle with the oil and cumin seeds, season with salt and black pepper, and bake in a preheated oven, at 400°F, for 25 minutes.

- Crumble over some feta or goat cheese to serve.

10 Red Pepper Hummus

Put 1 (15 oz) can chickpeas, rinsed and drained, into a food processor and add the juice of ½ lemon, 2 crushed garlic cloves, 1 teaspoon ground cumin, 2 drained roasted red peppers from a jar, 2 tablespoons tahini paste, and 2–3 tablespoons olive oil. Blend until smooth, adding a little more olive oil if you want to loosen the texture. Serve with vegetable crudités.

20 Peperonata

Heat 3 tablespoons olive oil in a saucepan over medium heat, add 2 sliced garlic cloves and 2 sliced onions, and cook for 1–2 minutes. Add 4 seeded and sliced red bell peppers and cook for another 10 minutes, then stir in 3 chopped, ripe tomatoes, and cook for 8 minutes. Stir in a few torn basil leaves and a sprinkling of pepper to serve.

20 Salmon Blinis

Serves 4

1½ cups buckwheat flour
2 teaspoons gluten-free
  baking powder
2 eggs
1¼ cups milk
1 tablespoon olive oil
⅓ cup crème fraîche
  or sour cream
1 tablespoon creamed horseradish
8 oz smoked salmon,
  cut into strips
black pepper
dill sprigs, to serve

- Sift the flour and baking powder into a bowl, then whisk in the eggs and milk to make a smooth batter.

- Heat the oil in a skillet over medium heat and spoon in tablespoons of the batter to make 1½–1¾ inch pancakes (the number you can make at one time will depend on the size of your pan). Cook until bubbles appear in the top and the underneath is cooked. Flip over and cook for 1–2 minutes on the other side. Repeat with the remaining batter.

- Mix together the crème fraîche or sour cream and creamed horseradish and divide the mixture among the pancakes.

- Top each one with smoked salmon and dust with black pepper. Serve topped with a dill sprig.

---

10 Salmon Toasts

Toast 4 slices of gluten-free bread for 2–3 minutes on each side. Stir 2 tablespoons chopped chives into 1 cup cream cheese, and spread the mixture onto the toast. Top the slices of toast with 8 oz smoked salmon strips and sprinkle with black pepper to serve.

30 Salmon Terrine

Line an 8½ x 4½ x 2½ inch loaf pan with plastic wrap. Arrange 3 oz strips of smoked salmon and a few dill sprigs in the bottom of the pan. In a food processor, process 3 oz smoked salmon, 3 oz poached salmon fillet, and 1 cup cream cheese until just mixed; do not overprocess. Stir in another

2 oz chopped smoked salmon, 3 oz flaked poached salmon fillet, ½ tablespoon chopped dill, and 2 sliced scallions. Spoon the mixture into the prepared pain and put into the refrigerator. Toast 4 gluten-free slices of bread or halved bagels and serve spread with the terrine.

Chicken Salad Wraps

Serves 4

4 gluten-free tortillas, warmed
¼ cup mayonnaise
4 teaspoons mango chutney
2 carrots, shredded
2 cooked chicken breasts, shredded
¼ small cabbage, thinly shredded
2 tomatoes, sliced
small handful of cilantro leaves
salt and black pepper

- Lay the tortillas on the work surface and spread each one with 1 tablespoon of the mayonnaise and 1 tablespoon of the mango chutney.

- Divide the remaining ingredients among the tortillas and season with salt and black pepper. Roll up the wraps to serve.

Chicken Club Sandwich

Broil 8 unsmoked bacon slices under a preheated hot broiler for 3–4 minutes on each side until crisp. Toast 12 slices of gluten-free bread for 2–3 minutes on each side. Spread 4 slices of the toast with 2 tablespoons mayonnaise. Top the slices with some shredded iceberg lettuce, 3 sliced tomatoes, and the bacon. Spread 4 more slices of toast with 2 tablespoons mango chutney and place on top of the bacon. Cover the mango with 2 sliced cooked chicken breasts and 1 thinly sliced small red onion. Top with the remaining slices of toast and secure each sandwich with 2 toothpicks. Slice in half diagonally to serve.

Chicken and Mango Quesadillas

Dived 2 cups shredded cheddar cheese evenly, sprinkling it over 4 gluten-free tortillas, then top with 2 cups cooked and sliced chicken breast. Sprinkle with 1 diced red onion, 2 sliced jalapeno chiles, 1 peeled, pitted, and diced mango, and a small handful of cilantro leaves. Spread 4 more tortillas with 1 tablespoon sour cream each and place them, cream side down, on the chicken tortillas. Heat ½ tablespoon olive oil in a skillet over medium heat, add one of the double tortillas to the pan, and cook for 3–4 minutes, until crisp and golden underneath. Carefully turn over and cook for another 2 minutes. Remove and keep warm, then repeat with the remaining quesadillas. Cut into wedges to serve.

10 Grilled Asparagus with Poached Eggs

Serves 4

1½ lb asparagus spears
1 tablespoon olive oil
4 eggs
2 oz Parmesan cheese

- Snap the woody ends off the asparagus spears and discard. Heat a ridged grill pan until hot and sprinkle it with the oil.

- Meanwhile, bring a skillet of water to a boil for the eggs.

- Place the asparagus on the grill pan and cook, turning regularly, until slightly charred at the ends.

- Stir the boiling water vigorously, then, one at a time, drop the cracked eggs into the center—the swirling water will help the egg white collect around the yolk and maintain the shape of the egg. Cook for 4–5 minutes, then remove with a slotted spoon.

- Place the asparagus on 4 warm plates and top with the poached eggs.

- Using a vegetable peeler, make curly shavings of Parmesan and sprinkle on top of the asparagus.

2 Asparagus Omelet

Heat 1 tablespoon oil in a skillet, add 6 chopped asparagus spears, 2 sliced scallions, and 3–4 sliced cremini mushrooms, and cook for 5–6 minutes. Whisk together 5 eggs and ¼ cup milk and pour into the pan, tipping the pan and moving the egg with a spatula to make sure it all cooks. Sprinkle with ¼ cup grated Parmesan, then place under a preheated hot broiler for 1–2 minutes, until golden. Cut into quarters and serve with a green salad and new potatoes.

3 Asparagus and Poached Egg Salad

Cook 8 oz new potatoes in a saucepan of boiling water for 12–15 minutes, until tender. Drain. Snap the woody ends off 12 oz asparagus spears and discard. Toss the asparagus and potatoes with 2 tablespoons olive oil. Heat a ridged grill pan until hot and cook the asparagus and potatoes in the pan for 4–5 minutes, until slightly charred; you may have to do this in batches. Poach 4 eggs in a skillet of simmering water for 4–5 minutes. Whisk together 3 tablespoons extra virgin olive oil, 1 tablespoon lemon juice, ½ teaspoon mustard, and 1 teaspoon honey. Toss the dressing with the asparagus, potatoes, and a bag of baby salad greens. Divide among 4 plates and top each one with a poached egg and a sprinkling of Parmesan shavings.

30 Herb Oat Cakes

Serves 4

2¼ cups rolled oats
3 sprigs rosemary, leaves only
1 cup gluten-free flour blend
1 teaspoon gluten-free
  baking powder
pinch of salt
6 tablespoons unsalted butter,
  cubed
½ cup milk
apples and cheese, to serve

- Put the oats and rosemary into a food processor and process until they start to break down and the mixture resembles bread crumbs.

- Add the flour, baking powder, and salt and blend again.

- Add the butter and process until it is mixed in, then pour in the milk while the machine is running and process until the dough comes together in a ball.

- Turn out onto a lightly floured work surface and roll out to a thickness of about ¼ inch. Cut out 20–24 circles, using a 2 inch cutter, rerolling as necessary, and place on a baking sheet.

- Bake in a preheated oven, at 375°F, for 12–15 minutes, until just starting to turn golden at the edges.

- Cool on a wire rack and serve with cheese and apples. Store in an airtight container.

 Quick Herb Oat Cakes

Combine 2 tablespoons olive oil with ¼ cup boiling water, then mix in 2⅓ cups oat bran with ¼ teaspoon salt and ½ tablespoon finely chopped rosemary. Work the mixture into a dough and roll out on a work surface sprinkled with oat bran. Cut out 20–24 shapes, using a knife or a cutter, and cook in a skillet over medium heat for 5 minutes on one side and 4 minutes on the other.

 Smoked Salmon Pâté on Quick Herb Oatcakes Follow the recipe for Quick Herb Oat Cakes, substituting dill for the rosemary. Then put 5 oz smoked salmon, 2 tablespoons chopped dill, the grated zest and juice of 1 lemon, 2 tablespoons heavy cream, ⅓ cup cream cheese, and freshly ground black pepper into a blender and blend until smooth. Spread the pâté on the oat cakes and serve topped with snipped chives.

10 Shrimp with Spicy Dip

Serves 4

1 cup cream cheese
½ cup plain yogurt
1 garlic clove, crushed
2–3 drops lemon juice
¼ teaspoon dried red
  pepper flakes
handful of snipped chives
2 small butterhead lettuce,
  leaves separated
12 oz jumbo shrimp,
  cooked and peeled
salt and black pepper

- To make the spicy dip, mix together the cream cheese, yogurt, garlic, lemon juice, red pepper flakes, and chives. Season with salt and black pepper to taste.

- Arrange the lettuce leaves on 4 small plates and top with the shrimp. Serve the dip in a bowl for everyone to share.

2 Spicy Shrimp Salad

Heat 2 tablespoons olive oil in a saucepan, add 1 tablespoon dried red pepper flakes and 2 crushed garlic cloves, and cook for 2 minutes. Add 1 lb peeled jumbo shrimp to the pan and cook for another 5–6 minutes, until the shrimp turn pink and are cooked through. Add a splash of white wine and cook until it has evaporated. Remove from the heat. Toss 3 cups arugula leaves in 2 tablespoons olive oil and 1 tablespoon balsamic vinegar. Divide among 4 plates and top with 2 sliced avocados. Spoon the shrimp over the salad and serve sprinkled with 1 tablespoon toasted sesame seeds.

3 Spicy Shrimp Curry

In a small blender, blend together 2 seeded red chiles, 1 small chopped red onion, a ¾ inch piece of fresh ginger root, peeled and grated, and 2–3 tablespoons water to create a smooth paste. Heat 1 tablespoon vegetable oil in a saucepan, add 1 tablespoon mustard seeds, ½ teaspoon fenugreek seeds, and 6 curry leaves, and cook until the mustard seeds begin to pop. Stir in the paste and ½ teaspoon turmeric and cook for another 2–3 minutes, then add 1 lb peeled jumbo shrimp. Pour in 1¾ cups coconut milk and bring to a simmer. Cook for 6–8 minutes, until the shrimp are pink and cooked through. Stir in 2 tablespoons chopped cilantro leaves. Serve the curry with cooked long-grain rice and a squeeze of lime juice.

10 Duck and Lettuce Wraps

Serves 4

6 scallions
2 cooked duck legs
2 small butterhead lettuce
½ cucumber, cut into thin strips
¼–⅓ cup gluten-free
  hoisin sauce
2 tablespoons roasted peanuts,
  coarsely chopped

- Cut the scallions into long, thin strips and put into a bowl of iced water for 4–5 minutes.

- Shred the meat from the duck legs.

- Separate the lettuce leaves and divide the shredded duck among them.

- Garnish each one with cucumber and scallion, spoon a little hoisin sauce over the top, and sprinkle with the chopped peanuts to serve.

---

20 Duck, Orange, and Watercress Salad

Heat 1 tablespoon vegetable oil in a wok over high heat, add the shredded meat from 2 duck legs, 1 teaspoon Chinese five spice powder, and 6 thickly sliced scallions, and stir-fry for 4–5 minutes. Remove from the pan and let cool. Whisk together 3 tablespoons extra virgin olive oil, 1 teaspoon sesame oil, 1 tablespoon rice vinegar, 1 teaspoon tamari soy sauce, and the finely grated zest and juice of 1 orange. Toss together 2 segmented oranges, ¾ bunch of watercress, 1 cup sliced radishes, the leaves of 2 endive heads, and the cooked spiced duck. Sprinkle with the dressing and 1 tablespoon chopped roasted peanuts.

30 Duck Satay with Peanut Sauce

Put ¼ cup firmly packed dark brown sugar, ½ cup soy sauce, ½ cup sherry, 2 star anise, 1 cinnamon stick, 1 split red chile, and ½ cup water in a saucepan over medium heat and bring to a boil, then remove from the heat and let cool for a few minutes. Pour the marinade over 4 skinless duck breasts and marinate for 15 minutes. Remove the duck from the marinade and pour ½ cup of the marinade into a saucepan with ¾ cup smooth peanut butter. Cook over low heat for 5 minutes. Cut the duck breast into strips and thread onto wooden skewers that have been soaked in water to prevent them from burning. Mix 2 tablespoons of the peanut sauce with 2 tablespoons olive oil and paint the mixture over the duck satay. Place under a preheated hot broiler and cook for 10–12 minutes, turning regularly, until golden. Serve with the remaining peanut sauce.

3⬤ Carrot and Lentil Muffins

Serves 4

⅓ cup red lentils

2¼ cups gluten-free flour blend

2 tablespoons ground flaxseed

1½ teaspoons gluten-free
baking powder

¼ cup firmly packed light
brown sugar

1 teaspoon ground cinnamon

½ teaspoon ground cloves

3 tablespoons applesauce

3 tablespoons honey

3 tablespoons sunflower oil

1 egg

1 large carrot, peeled and
shredded

2–3 tablespoons soy milk
(optional)

- Line a 12-section muffin pan with paper liners.

- Cook the red split lentils in 1¼ cups water for 8 minutes, until soft. Drain.

- Sift the flour, flaxseed, and baking powder into a large bowl then stir in the sugar and spices.

- Put the lentils into a food processor with the applesauce, honey, oil, and egg and blend until smooth.

- Pour the wet ingredients into the dry, stirring in the shredded carrots when nearly blended. Add the soy milk to loosen the batter, if needed.

- Spoon into the muffin liners and bake in a preheated oven, at 350°F, for 18–20 minutes, until risen and golden. Cool on a rack.

1⬤ **Carrot and
Lentil Salad**

Blanch 6 peeled carrots cut into batons in boiling water for 3–4 minutes, then refresh under cold running water. Toss with 1 (15 oz) can, rinsed and drained, or 2 cups cooked green lentils 1 seeded and diced red bell pepper, 1 thinly sliced small red onion, and 2 cups mâche. Whisk together 3 tablespoons olive oil, 1 tablespoon white wine vinegar, 1 teaspoon cumin seeds, 1 teaspoon honey, and ½ teaspoon Dijon mustard and pour over the salad to serve.

2⬤ **Carrot and
Lentil Soup**

Dry-fry 2 teaspoons cumin seeds and a pinch of dried red pepper flakes in a small skillet for 1 minute. Heat 1 tablespoon olive oil in a saucepan, then add half of the spices, 10 peeled and shredded carrots, ¾ cup red lentils, 4 cups vegetable stock, and ½ cup milk to the pan and bring to a boil. Simmer for 12–15 minutes, until the lentils are soft and swollen. Using a handheld blender, blend the soup until smooth. Serve with

a drizzle of plain yogurt, a few cilantro leaves, and the remaining spices sprinkled over the top.

 # Chicken and Vegetable Satay

Serves 4

½ cup tamari soy sauce

3 tablespoons smooth
  peanut butter

2 chicken breasts, cut into strips

4 large mushrooms, halved

1 red bell pepper, seeded and
  cut into chunks

1 yellow bell pepper, seeded
  and cut into chunks

1 zucchini, halved and sliced

½ napa lettuce, shredded

2 carrots, peeled and grated

¼ cup bean sprouts

small handful of cilantro leaves

2 teaspoons sesame oil

juice of 1 lime

2 tablespoons sesame seeds,
  toasted, to serve

- In a large bowl, mix together the tamari, peanut butter, and 2 tablespoons water.

- Toss the chicken and mushrooms, bell peppers, and zucchini in the peanut mixture and thread onto 8 satay sticks that have been soaked in water to prevent them from burning.

- Place under a preheated hot broiler and cook for 12–14 minutes, turning regularly, until the chicken is cooked through.

- Meanwhile, toss together the lettuce, shredded carrot, bean sprouts, and cilantro leaves with the sesame oil and lime juice.

- Serve the satay with the salad, sprinkled with toasted sesame seeds.

 ### Chicken Satay with Satay Sauce

Stir-fry 1½ cups peanuts in ½ cup vegetable oil for 1 minute, then blend until smooth. Sauté 2 chopped garlic cloves and 4 chopped shallots for 30 seconds, then add 1 tablespoon tamari soy sauce, 1 teaspoon brown sugar, 1 diced red chile, 1¾ cups water, and the blended peanuts and simmer for 7–8 minutes to thicken. Meanwhile, broil 8 prepared chicken satay sticks for 3–4 minutes on each side. Stir the juice of 1 lemon into the satay sauce and serve with the chicken.

 ### Chicken Satay Drumsticks

Mix together 1 tablespoon tamari soy sauce, 1 tablespoon honey, 1 teaspoon turmeric, 1 teaspoon ground cumin, 2 crushed garlic cloves, 2 teaspoons grated fresh ginger root, the juice of ½ lime, and 1 tablespoon sunflower oil. Pierce 8 chicken drumsticks several times with a sharp knife, put into an ovenproof dish, and pour the marinade over them. Bake in a preheated oven, at 400°F, for 25–30 minutes. Meanwhile, put ⅓ cup chunky peanut butter,

1 teaspoon Thai red curry paste, ½ cup coconut milk, 2 teaspoons packed dark brown sugar, and the juice of ½ lime in a small saucepan and bring to a simmer. Cook for 4–5 minutes, until thickened. Serve the chicken wings sprinkled with 1 tablespoon chopped cilantro leaves, with the peanut sauce on the side.

Fusilli with Sun-Dried Tomatoes and Artichokes

Serves 4

12 oz gluten-free fusilli
2 tablespoons extra virgin olive oil
1 tablespoon balsamic vinegar
½ teaspoon Dijon mustard
½ teaspoon honey
1 garlic clove, crushed
10 sun-dried tomatoes, sliced
1 (14 oz) can artichoke hearts,
  drained and halved
4 oz Parmesan cheese shavings

- Cook the fusilli in a saucepan of boiling water for 9–12 minutes, or according to the package directions.

- Whisk together the oil, vinegar, mustard, honey, and garlic to make the dressing.

- Drain the pasta and return to the pan with the dressing. Stir in the sun-dried tomatoes and artichoke hearts and warm through.

- Serve in shallow pasta bowls, sprinkled with the Parmesan shavings.

Artichoke and Sun-Dried Tomato Bruschetta Slice 2 gluten-free baguettes into 16 slices and place on a baking sheet. Drizzle with 2 tablespoons olive oil and toast for 2–3 minutes on each side. Rub one side of each slice with a garlic clove. Top the bruschettta with a 1 (14 oz) can artichoke hearts, drained and sliced, 12 chopped sun-dried tomatoes, and 12 torn slices of prosciutto. Serve sprinkled with 2 tablespoons toasted pine nuts and small basil leaves.

Tomato, Artichoke, and Prosciutto Pizzas Spread 2 gluten-free pizza crusts with 1 (14½ oz) can of diced tomatoes, going up to the edges. Top with a 1 (14 oz) can of artichoke hearts, drained and cut in half, 14 halved sun-dried tomatoes, 6–8 torn basil leaves, and 6 slices prosciutto, finishing with 6 oz sliced mozzarella. Bake in a preheated oven, at 425°F, until golden and bubbling.

3⊙ Spicy Turkey Burgers with Red Pepper Salsa

Serves 4

1 lb ground turkey

¾ inch piece of fresh ginger root, peeled and grated

4 scallions, finely chopped

1 red chile, seeded and finely chopped

1 egg yolk

2 tablespoons chopped cilantro

4 small butterhead lettuce

For the salsa

1 red bell pepper, seeded and diced

1 tomato, diced

1 small red onion, finely diced

½ tablespoon chopped parsley

½ tablespoon chopped cilantro

1 tablespoon red wine vinegar

½ tablespoon olive oil

- Mix together the ground turkey, ginger, scallions, chile, egg yolk, and cilantro.

- Using wet hands, shape the mixture into 4 patties.

- Heat a lightly oiled skillet and cook the patties for 5–6 minutes on either side, until golden and cooked through.

- Meanwhile, for the salsa, mix together the bell pepper, tomatoes, onion, parsley, cilantro, vinegar, and oil.

- Serve the burgers on a bed of lettuce, topped with the salsa.

1⊙ Spiced Turkey-Stuffed Pitas

Toast 4 gluten-free pita breads for 2–3 minutes on each side. Cut along one edge to open like a pocket. Spread each pita with ½ tablespoon each mayonnaise and mango chutney. Divide ¼ shredded iceberg lettuce, 4 sliced tomatoes, 2 cups sliced cooked turkey, and 1 small thinly sliced red onion among the pitas, top each with ½ tablespoon prepared salsa, and sprinkle with some chopped cilantro to serve.

2⊙ Asian Turkey Salad

Mix together 3 finely sliced shallots with ¼ teaspoon salt and let stand for 10 minutes. Whisk together the juice of 1 lime, 2 tablespoons Thai fish sauce, 1 tablespoon rice vinegar, 1 tablespoon granulated sugar, 2 crushed garlic cloves, and 1 finely diced red chile. In a large bowl, toss together 2 cups cooked turkey strips, 4 cups finely shredded napa cabbage, 1 large peeled and shredded carrot, 1 cup bean sprouts, and a small handful each of mint and basil. Toss in the shallots and dressing and let stand for 5 minutes, then serve sprinkled with ⅓ cup chopped roasted peanuts.

10 Egg-Filled Mushrooms on Toast

Serves 4

2 tablespoons butter

4 eggs, beaten

½ tablespoon chives, chopped

1 tablespoon olive oil

4 portobello mushrooms

4 slices of gluten-free bread, toasted

2 tomatoes, chopped

2 scallions, thinly sliced

salt and black pepper

- Melt the butter in a small skillet. Pour in the eggs and chives, season with salt and black pepper, and cook for 4–5 minutes, stirring occasionally, until cooked.

- Meanwhile, heat the oil in a skillet and cook the mushrooms for 3–4 minutes on each side.

- Mix together the tomatoes and scallions.

- Place the toast on 4 warm plates and top with the mushrooms, then drizzle over any pan juices.

- Spoon the scrambled egg into the mushrooms and serve sprinkled with the tomato and scallion mixture.

---

20 Poached Egg-Topped Mushroom Soup

Soup Put 1 oz dried porcini in a bowl, cover with boiling water, and soak for 3–4 minutes. Meanwhile, heat 2 tablespoons olive oil in a large saucepan, add 12 oz assorted wild or cremini mushrooms, 2 crushed garlic cloves, a few thyme leaves, and 1 diced red onion and cook for 6–8 minutes. Add the soaked porcini and strained liquid along with 4 cups vegetable stock and simmer for 6–8 minutes. Blend the soup, using a handheld blender, until smooth. Poach 4 eggs in a skillet of simmering water for 4–5 minutes. Serve the soup in warm bowls with the eggs and a sprinkling of chopped parsley.

30 Mushroom and Egg Pizzas

Heat 2 tablespoons olive oil in a saucepan over medium heat, add 1 sliced red onion, 2 sliced garlic cloves, and 3 cups sliced cremini mushrooms, and cook for 5 minutes. Put 2 gluten-free pizza crusts on baking sheets and spread with ¾ cup prepared tomato pizza topping, then sprinkle with 3 cups baby spinach leaves and spoon the mushrooms over the top. Crack 2 eggs on each pizza, one on each half, and top with ¾ cup shredded mozzarella. Bake in a preheated oven, at 425°F, for 22–25 minutes, until golden and bubbling. Serve with a salad.

Broiled Sardines with Pan-Fried Lemon Potatoes

Serves 4

1¼ lb new potatoes, thickly sliced
1 tablespoon olive oil
12 sardines, cleaned and gutted
grated zest and juice of 1 lemon
2 tablespoons chopped parsley

- Cook the potatoes in boiling water for 12–15 minutes, until tender.

- Heat the oil in a skillet over medium heat, add the potatoes, and cook for 6–8 minutes, turning regularly, until golden.

- Meanwhile, place the sardines in a broiler pan and pour the lemon juice over them. Cook the sardines under a preheated hot broiler for 2–3 minutes on each side.

- Toss the lemon zest and chopped parsley into the potatoes and serve with the broiled sardines.

Broiled Sardines on Toast

Cook 8 cleaned and gutted sardines under a preheated hot broiler for 2–3 minutes on each side. Meanwhile, toast 4 slices of gluten-free bread. Mix together 3 sliced scallions, 1 tablespoon chopped parsley, and the grated zest of 1 lemon. Season. Place 2 sardines on each slice of toast, spoon the herb mixture over them, and drizzle with olive oil and lemon juice.

Marinated Sardine Bruschetta

Place 12 butterflied sardines in a shallow dish with the juice and zest of 1 lemon, 4 sliced garlic cloves, 2 torn bay leaves, 1 sliced red chile, and 1¾ cups white wine vinegar. Let marinate for 20 minutes. Meanwhile, slice 2 gluten-free baguettes into 12 thick slices, put on a baking sheet, and drizzle with 2 tablespoons olive oil. Toast each side for 2–3 minutes, then rub one side of each slice with a garlic clove. Heat a ridged grill pan until hot and cook the sardines for 1 minute on each side. Serve the sardines on the toasted bruschetta with a sprinkling of chopped parsley.

 Corned Beef Hash

Serves 4

5 red-skinned or white round potatoes, peeled
1 tablespoon olive oil
1 onion, chopped
1 (12 oz) can corned beef
2 tomatoes, chopped
dash of Worcestershire sauce
2 tablespoons butter or olive oil
4 eggs

- Cook the potatoes in boiling water for 12–14 minutes, until tender.

- Meanwhile, heat the oil in a large skillet, add the onion, and cook for 4–5 minutes.

- Add the corned beef to the pan and cook for another 2–3 minutes.

- Drain the potatoes and add them to the pan, cooking and lightly crushing them for 1–2 minutes. Stir in the tomatoes and Worcestershire sauce and cook for another 3–4 minutes.

- Meanwhile, heat the butter or oil in another skillet and cook the eggs to your preference.

- Serve the corned beef hash topped with a fried egg.

 Corned Beef, Egg, and Salad Baguette

Slice 4 gluten-free baguettes in half horizontally and toast each piece for 2–3 minutes on each side. Spread the bottom half of each baguette with 1 tablespoon chutney. Top with ¼ shredded iceberg lettuce, 1 sliced hard-boiled egg, and one-quarter of 1 (12 oz) can of corned beef, sliced. Sandwich together with the remaining baguettes.

 Corned Beef Casserole

Cook 5 peeled and chopped russet potatoes in boiling water for 12–15 minutes, until tender. Meanwhile, heat 1 tablespoon olive oil in a saucepan over medium heat, add 1 diced onion, 1 diced celery stick, and 1 peeled and diced carrot, and cook for 3–4 minutes. Add 12 oz ground beef and brown for 3–4 minutes, then stir in 1 (12 oz) can of corned beef. Pour in ½ cup red wine and simmer for 12–15 minutes. Put into an ovenproof dish. Drain the potatoes and mash with 2 tablespoons butter, ⅔ cup crumbled feta cheese, and 1 tablespoon chopped parsley. Spread the potatoes over the meat and cook in a preheated oven, at 400°F, for 12 minutes. Serve with steamed cabbage.

1 Mackerel Pâté with Steamed Broccoli Quinoa

Serves 4

1¼ cups quinoa
4 cups broccoli florets
2 (8 oz) smoked mackerel fillets
2 scallions, finely chopped
1 teaspoon horseradish sauce
⅓ cup sour cream
6 cups baby spinach leaves

- Put the quinoa into a saucepan, cover with boiling water, and cook for 8–9 minutes, or according to the package directions.

- Meanwhile, steam the broccoli florets for 4–5 minutes.

- Skin the mackerel, put into a bowl, and break up the flakes with a fork. Add the scallions, horseradish, and sour cream and mix well to form a pâté.

- Drain the quinoa, refresh under cold running water, and drain again. Toss together with the broccoli.

- Divide the spinach leaves among 4 plates and top with the quinoa and then the pâté to serve.

---

2 Mackerel with Caramelized Red Onion

Heat 1 tablespoon olive oil in a saucepan over medium heat, add 2 sliced red onions, and cook for 2–3 minutes, stirring constantly. Cover and cook for another 3–4 minutes. Stir in 2 teaspoons balsamic vinegar, then cover and cook for another 7–8 minutes, until the onions are soft and starting to caramelize. Meanwhile, cook ½ cup quinoa in boiling water according to the package directions. Drain and refresh under running cold water then drain again. Heat ½ tablespoon olive oil in a skillet, add 4 mackerel fillets, skin side down, and cook for 3–4 minutes, then turn over and cook for another 3–4 minutes; do not overcook. Toss together 5 prepared cooked beets, cut into wedges, the quinoa, 3½ cups arugula leaves, and 1 tablespoon salad dressing of your choice. Serve each fillet on a bed of caramelized onions with the salad on the side.

3 Mackerel with Quinoa Salad

Score 4 whole mackerel 3 times on each side with a knife. Cook 1 teaspoon each of cumin, turmeric, and ground coriander in 1 tablespoon olive oil for 1–2 minutes. Brush the spiced oil over the fish. Cook ½ cup quinoa according to the package directions. Drain and refresh under cold running water, then drain again. Mix together the quinoa, 2 finely sliced scallions, ½ diced red bell pepper, 2 diced tomatoes, 2 tablespoons chopped cilantro leaves, 1 teaspoon lemon juice, black pepper, and ½ tablespoon olive oil. Cook the fish under a hot broiler for 7–8 minutes on each side until cooked through. Serve with the quinoa salad.

2 Corn Fritters

Serves 4

1⅔ cups gluten-free flour blend

1¾ teaspoons gluten-free baking powder

1 egg, beaten

⅔ cup milk

1⅓ cups corn kernels (drained, if canned, or thawed, if frozen)

1 tablespoon olive oil

4 eggs

salt and black pepper

snipped chives, to serve

- Put the flour into a large bowl and whisk in the egg and milk to make a smooth batter.

- Stir in the corn and season with salt and black pepper.

- Heat the oil in a skillet over medium heat, spoon in tablespoons of the batter (the number of fritters you can make at one time will depend on the size of your pan), and cook for 2–3 minutes on each side, until golden. Repeat with the remaining batter.

- Meanwhile, poach the eggs in a skillet of simmering water for 4–5 minutes.

- Serve a few fritters topped with a poached egg and a sprinkling of chopped chives.

1 Corn Soup

Heat 2 tablespoons olive oil in a saucepan over medium heat and add 1 diced onion and 2 peeled and diced red-skinned potatoes. Cook for 1–2 minutes, then pour in 4 cups hot vegetable stock. Simmer for 5 minutes, until the potato is soft. Stir in 2⅔ cups corn kernels and cook for another 2 minutes. Stir in ½ cup light cream and, using a handheld blender, blend half of the soup, leaving the remainder chunky, and mix together. Serve with a sprinkling of chopped chives.

3 Corn and Potato Frittata

Cook 5 peeled and sliced red-skinned or white round potatoes in a large saucepan of boiling water for 2–3 minutes, until tender. Drain. Heat 2 tablespoons olive oil in a heatproof skillet, add 1 sliced onion and 1 seeded and diced red pepper, and cook for 2–3 minutes, then remove with a slotted spoon. Beat 8 eggs in a large bowl and stir in the potato mixture, 2⅔ cups corn kernels, and 2 tablespoons chopped parsley, and season well with salt and black pepper. Heat another tablespoon olive oil in the skillet and gently pour in the egg mixture, moving the ingredients around a little as the egg starts to cook. Continue to cook over low heat for 12–15 minutes, until the underneath is golden. Sprinkle with ½ cup shredded cheddar cheese and place the skillet under a preheated hot broiler for 5–6 minutes, until golden and bubbling. Turn the frittata out onto a board and cut into wedges to serve.

Barbecued Vegetable Kebabs with Herb Dipping Sauce

Serves 4

3 red onions, cut into wedges

2 zucchini, thickly sliced

2 red bell peppers, seeded and chopped

1 yellow bell pepper, seeded and chopped

¼ cup olive oil

1 tablespoon balsamic vinegar

2 tablespoons chopped fresh herbs

salt and black pepper

- Thread the vegetables alternately onto 8 bamboo skewers that have been presoaked in cold water to prevent them from burning.

- Brush the vegetables with 1 tablespoon of the oil and season well with salt and black pepper.

- Place the kebabs under a preheated hot broiler or on a barbecue grill for 12–15 minutes, turning regularly.

- Meanwhile, make the dipping sauce. Mix together the remaining oil, vinegar, and herbs in a small bowl.

- Serve the vegetable kebabs with the herb dipping sauce.

Quick Vegetable and Herb Soup

Heat 1 tablespoon olive oil in a saucepan over medium heat, add 1 large chopped onion, 2 sliced garlic cloves, 3 sliced celery sticks, and 2 cups finely diced butternut squash, and cook for 2–3 minutes. Pour in 1 (14½ oz) can of diced tomatoes and 2½ cups hot vegetable stock and bring to a boil. Simmer for 7–8 minutes, then stir in 2 tablespoons chopped parsley. Season the soup with salt and black pepper to taste and serve.

Roasted Vegetables with Quinoa Herb Salad

In a large roasting pan, toss together the wedges from ¼ of a butternut squash, 2 red onions cut into wedges, 6 trimmed baby leeks, 4 garlic cloves, and 2 large peeled and chopped carrots. Sprinkle with some salt and black pepper, 2 tablespoons olive oil, and 1 tablespoon coriander seeds and roasted in a preheated oven, at 400°F, for 25 minutes. Meanwhile, cook 1¼ cups quinoa in a saucepan of boiling water for 8–9 minutes according to the package directions, then drain and refresh under cold running water and drain again. Place in a bowl and mix with ½ diced cucumber, 4 diced tomatoes, the grated zest of 1 lemon, 6 finely sliced scallions, ⅓ cup finely chopped parsley, and ½ cup finely chopped mint. Stir in 2 tablespoons extra virgin olive oil. Pan-fry 8 oz thickly sliced halloumi, mozzarella, or Muenster cheese for 3–4 minutes on each side, until golden. Spoon the quinoa salad onto a large plate, spoon the roasted vegetables on top, and finish with the cheese.

Grapefruit and Sea Bass Tacos

Serves 4

1 lb sea bass fillet
1 grapefruit, ½ juiced and
 ½ segmented and chopped
1 red chile, seeded and thinly
 sliced
4 scallions, sliced
1 tablespoon chopped cilantro
8 taco shells
2 small butterhead lettuce

- Thinly slice the sea bass fillets and put into a nonmetallic bowl with the grapefruit juice and segments, chile, scallions, and cilantro. Mix well.

- Heat the taco shells according to the package directions. Shred the lettuce and add halve to the bottom of each taco and then spoon in the sea bass mixture to serve.

 Pan-Fried Sea Bass with Grapefruit-Dressed Broccoli

Cook 5 cups broccoli florets in a saucepan of boiling water for 2 minutes, then drain. Heat 2 tablespoons olive oil in a skillet, add the broccoli, and cook for 2–3 minutes. Remove from the heat and stir in the segments of 2 pink grapefruit. Transfer to a bowl and pour 2 tablespoons grapefruit juice over the top. Season. Score the skin of 4 (5 oz) sea bass fillets. Heat 2 tablespoons olive oil in a skillet, add the fillets, skin side down, and cook for 3–4 minutes on each side. Transfer to 4 warm plates, then add 2 tablespoons capers and 6 coarsely chopped anchovies to the pan and cook until they start to crisp. Serve the sea bass fillets on a bed of broccoli and grapefruit, with the capers spooned over the top.

Sea Bass and Grapefruit Salad

In a small blender or mortar and pestle, grind together 1 tablespoon paprika, 2 chopped garlic cloves, 1 tablespoon extra virgin olive oil, ½ tablespoon chili powder, 1 teaspoon dried oregano, ½ teaspoon allspice, and 3 tablespoons grapefruit juice. Rub the mixture over 4 (5 oz) sea bass fillets and let marinate for 15 minutes. Meanwhile, whisk together ⅓ cup grapefruit juice, 3 tablespoons extra virgin olive oil, 1 tablespoon chopped mint and 1 tablespoon chopped fresh ginger root. Toss together 1 (12 oz) package salad greens with 2 segmented pink grapefruits, 1 peeled, pitted, and chopped mango, and 1 peeled, pitted, and sliced avocado. Cook the fish under a preheated hot broiler for 3–4 minutes on each side. Toss the dressing with the salad, divide among 4 plates. and top each one with a sea bass fillet.

 Savory Crepes

Serves 4

8 carrots, peeled and chopped
1 (15 oz) can lima beans, rinsed
 and drained
¾ cup rice flour
1 teaspoon gluten-free
 baking powder
1 egg
¾ cup soy milk
2 teaspoons olive oil
½ cup walnuts, toasted
2 tablespoons chopped parsley
¾ cup shredded cheddar cheese
salt and black pepper
crisp green salad, to serve

- Cook the carrots in boiling water for 6–8 minutes, then add the lima beans and cook for another 2 minutes.

- Meanwhile, in a food processor, blend together the flour, baking powder, egg, milk, and 2–3 tablespoons water until you have a runny batter.

- Heat a lightly oiled skillet over medium heat, pour in one-quarter of the batter, and cook for 2–3 minutes on each side. Keep warm and repeat with the remaining batter.

- Crush the carrots and lima beans, then stir in the walnuts and parsley. Season with salt and black pepper.

- Divide the carrot mixture among the crepes, placing it in the middle and then folding over each crepe.

- Place the crepes on a baking sheet, sprinkle with the cheddar, and cook under a preheated hot broiler for 3–4 minutes, until golden. Serve with a crisp green salad.

 Savory Drop Pancakes

Whisk 2 eggs with 1½ cups bluckwheat flour, 2 teaspoons gluten-free baking powder, and 1¼ cups milk to create a smooth batter. Heat 1 teaspoon olive oil in a skillet and pour in 4 separate tablespoons of the batter to make 4 small pancakes. Cook until small bubbles appear, then turn over and cook for another 1 minute. Repeat with the remaining batter. Top the pancakes with 1 cup arugula leaves, 1 cup hummus, and 2 peeled and shredded carrots.

 Ratatouille-Stuffed Crepes

Heat 1 tablespoon olive oil in a saucepan and add 1 diced eggplant, 1 seeded and chopped red bell pepper, 1 seeded and chopped yellow bell pepper, 1 sliced red onion, 2 sliced zucchini, a 1 (14½ oz) can of diced tomatoes, 1 cup water and ½ teaspoon dried oregano. Bring to a simmer and cook for 20 minutes. Meanwhile, make 4 crepes as in the recipe above. Divide the ratatouille among the crepes, roll them up, and place them in an ovenproof dish.

Pour 1¼ cups prepared heated cheese sauce over them, and sprinkle with ¾ cup shredded Gruyère or Swiss cheese, then cook under a preheated hot broiler for 3–4 minutes, until golden and bubbling.

3⦿ Salmon Ceviche

Serves 4

1 lb fresh salmon, thinly sliced
juice of 6–8 limes
4 scallions, finely chopped
2 celery sticks, finely sliced
1 tablespoon fresh cilantro,
  finely chopped
½ bunch of watercress, to garnish
oat cakes, to serve

- Put the salmon in a nonmetallic bowl and cover with the lime juice. Cover and let stand in the refrigerator for 25 minutes.

- When ready to serve, drain the salmon, add the scallions, celery, and cilantro, and mix well.

- Garnish with the watercress and serve with oat cakes.

Hot-Smoked Salmon Salad

Blanch 12 trimmed asparagus spears in a saucepan of boiling water for 1–2 minutes, then drain and refresh under cold running water. Whisk together 3 tablespoons extra virgin olive oil, 1 tablespoon lime juice, 1 teaspoon whole-grain mustard, ½ teaspoon honey, and 1 seeded and diced red chile. In a large bowl, toss together 12 oz flaked hot-smoked salmon, 4 sliced scallions, a small handful of cilantro leaves, 1 cup sliced radishes, 8 cups mixed salad greens, 12 halved baby plum tomatoes, the cooked asparagus, and the salad dressing. Serve immediately with lime wedges.

Salmon and Rice Noodle Stir-Fry

Cook 4 oz rice noodles according to the package directions. Heat 1 tablespoon olive oil in a wok and cook 12 oz sliced salmon fillet with 2 finely chopped garlic cloves for 2–3 minutes. Add 3 diced tomatoes and 4 sliced scallions and cook for another 1–2 minutes. Add 3 tablespoons tamari soy sauce, 1 tablespoon honey, the juice of 1 lime, and a small handful of cilantro leaves. Cook for 1–2 minutes. Divide the noodles among 4 bowls and top with the salmon. Sprinkle with 1 tablespoon sesame seeds and serve garnished with chopped chives.

 # Bean and Spinach Frittata

Serves 4

5 cups fava beans, fresh or frozen
¼ cup halved green beans
8 cups baby spinach leaves
6 extra-large eggs
small bunch of parsley, chopped
¾ cup grated Manchego or
   Parmesan cheese
2 tablespoons olive oil
salt and black pepper

- Blanch the fava beans in large saucepan of boiling water for 5–6 minutes, until tender. Let cool a little, then pop the beans out of their skins.

- Blanch the green beans in a saucepan of boiling water for 1–2 minutes, then drain and refresh under cold running water.

- Steam the spinach for 1–2 minutes, until wilted. Squeeze out any excess liquid.

- In a large bowl, beat the eggs with some salt and black pepper, then stir in the beans, spinach, parsley, and one-half of the cheese.

- Heat the oil in a skillet and pour in the egg mixture. Turn the heat down to low and cook for 10–12 minutes, until cooked underneath. Sprinkle the remaining cheese over the frittata and cook under a preheated medium broiler for 2 minutes, until golden.

- Turn out onto a board and cut into wedges to serve.

 ### Bean and Spinach Salad

Whisk together 3 tablespoons olive oil and ¼ cup lemon juice. Blanch 2 cups green beans and 3 cups fava beans in a saucepan of boiling water for 5–6 minutes. Drain and refresh under cold running water. Toss the beans with 4 cups baby spinach leaves, 3 chopped scallions, and 12 quartered baby plum tomatoes. Sprinkle with 1 cup crumbled feta cheese and drizzle with the dressing to serve.

 ### Bean and Spinach Stew

Heat 1 tablespoon vegetable oil in a saucepan over medium heat add 1 chopped onion and cook for 2–3 minutes. Stir in 3 teaspoons ground cumin and 2 crushed garlic cloves and cook for another 1–2 minutes. Stir in 1 (14½ oz) can of diced tomatoes and 2–3 tablespoons water and cook for 5 minutes. Add ¾ cup rinsed and drained, canned cannellini beans, 1⅓ cups fava beans, 1 cup trimmed green beans, and 1 tablespoon chopped basil and bring to a boil, then simmer for 20 minutes. Stir in 3½ cups baby spinach leaves and cook for another 2–3 minutes.

GLU-SNAC-SIR

1 Chicken and Tarragon Pesto Penne

Serves 4

12 oz gluten-free penne
½ cup olive oil
1 cup grated Parmesan cheese
handful of tarragon leaves
½ cup pine nuts, toasted
1 garlic clove, crushed
grated zest and juice of 1 lemon
3 cooked chicken breasts, sliced
½ bunch of watercress
12 baby tomatoes, quartered

- Cook the penne in a large saucepan of boiling water for 8–9 minutes, or according to the package directions. Drain and refresh under cold running water, then toss with 2 tablespoons of the oil.

- Meanwhile, put the Parmesan, tarragon, pine nuts, garlic, and lemon zest into a food processor and process for 1 minute. Then, while the machine is running, gradually pour in the remaining olive oil to form the pesto.

- Toss the pesto with the pasta, chicken, watercress, tomatoes, and lemon juice, and serve.

2 Chicken and TarragonTagliatelle

Toss 4 (5 oz) chicken breasts in 2 tablespoons olive oil with 2 tablespoons chopped tarragon seasoned with black pepper. Cook the chicken breasts under a preheated hot broiler for 5–6 minutes on each side, until cooked through. Meanwhile, cook 12 oz gluten-free tagliatelle for 9–12 minutes or according to the package directions. Heat 1 tablespoon olive oil in a large skillet over medium heat, add 4 chopped scallions and 12 quartered baby tomatoes, and cook for 2 minutes. Slice the chicken breasts and add to the pan. Drain the pasta and toss in the pan. Serve sprinkled with 2 tablespoons toasted pine nuts.

3 Chicken and Tarragon Pizza

Spread ¾ cup prepared pizza topping on 2 prepared gluten-free pizza crusts. Top each one with 3 sliced tomatoes, 1 seeded and sliced green bell pepper, 3 sliced cooked chicken breasts, and 5 oz sliced mozzarella. Drizzle with 1 tablespoon prepared pesto and sprinkle with 1 tablespoon chopped tarragon. Bake in a preheated oven, at 425°F, for 25 minutes, until golden and bubbling. Serve with a crisp green salad.

10 Broccoli and Anchovy Linguine

Serves 4

1 lb gluten-free linguine

4 cups broccoli florets

⅓ cup extra virgin olive oil

1 red chile, seeded and
   finely chopped

16 anchovies, chopped

- Cook the pasta in a large saucepan of boiling water for 9 minutes, or according to the package directions, adding the broccoli florets after 5 minutes.

- Drain the pasta and broccoli and keep warm.

- Meanwhile, heat the oil in a skillet over medium heat, add the chile and anchovies, and stir-fry for 2 minutes.

- Add the pasta and broccoli to the pan, stirring well to coat with the spicy oil. Serve immediately.

20 Quick Broccoli and Anchovy Pizza

Toast 4 gluten-free pita breads for 2 minutes on each side. Spread each one with 1½ tablespoons ketchup. Cook 4 cups broccoli florets in boiling water for 4–5 minutes, then drain. Heat 1 tablespoon olive oil in a skillet, add ½ tablespoon red pepper flakes and 12 chopped anchovies, and cook for 1 minute. Toss the broccoli in the anchovy mixture, then spoon them over the pita breads. Top with 1 cup crumbled feta cheese to serve.

30 Broccoli and Anchovy Pizza

Blanch 4 cups broccoli florets in boiling water for 3–4 minutes, then refresh under cold running water and drain. Spread 1⅓ cups pizza topping over 2 prepared gluten-free pizza crusts placed on baking sheets. Top with the broccoli, 12 chopped anchovies, and 2 sliced garlic cloves. Sprinkle with 1 cup grated mozzarella and bake in a preheated oven, at 425°F, for 20–22 minutes.

20 Eggs Florentine

Serves 4

1½ (10 oz) packages
  spinach leaves
1 tablespoon butter, melted
pinch of grated nutmeg
4 extra-large eggs
salt and black pepper

For the cheese sauce

1½ tablespoons butter
3 tablespoons gluten-free
  flour blend
¼ teaspoon smooth mustard
1¼ cups milk
¾ cup shredded sharp
  cheddar cheese

- To make the cheese sauce, melt the butter in a small saucepan, then stir in the flour and mustard. Cook, stirring continuously, for 1 minute.

- Pour in the milk gradually, whisking to remove any lumps, then cook over gentle heat, stirring continuously, until it begins to boil. Turn the heat down to a simmer and stir in two-thirds of the cheddar.

- Meanwhile, put the spinach in a saucepan with the melted butter and cook for a few minutes. Season with salt and black pepper, then add the nutmeg. Place in an ovenproof dish, or divide among 4 individual ovenproof dishes.

- Poach the eggs in a skillet of simmering water for 4–5 minutes, then drain and place them on top of the spinach.

- Pour the cheese sauce over the top and sprinkle with the remaining cheddar. Place under a preheated hot broiler and cook until golden and bubbling. Serve immediately.

 Egg, Bacon and Spinach Salad

Broil 4 slices of unsmoked bacon under a hot broiler until crisp, then chop coarsely. Toss together 5 cups spinach leaves with ¼ bunch of watercress, 4 chopped scallions, 12 halved baby tomatoes, and 2 tablespoons of prepared salad dressing. Poach 4 eggs in a skillet of simmering water for 4–5 minutes. Divide the salad among 4 plates and top each one with a poached egg and some crispy bacon.

 Egg and Spinach Omelet

Beat 8 eggs with some salt and black pepper and 1 tablespoon crème fraîche or heavy cream. Heat 1 tablespoon sunflower oil in a skillet over medium heat, pour one-quarter of the mixture into the pan, and swirl it around with a fork, tipping the pan from time to time so all of the egg mixture gets cooked. Sprinkle in 1 cup baby spinach leaves and ¼ cup shredded cheddar cheese and fold over half the omelet to nearly cover the spinach and cheese. Cook for another 1–2 minutes, then remove from the pan and keep warm. Repeat to make 4 omelets.

GLU-SNAC-FAL

30 Roasted Chicken, Red Pepper, and Sweet Potato

Serves 4

3 red bell peppers, seeded
and cut into wedges
2 sweet potatoes, peeled
and cut into wedges
2 red onions, cut into wedges
8–10 thyme sprigs
4 garlic cloves
3 tablespoons olive oil
4 chicken breasts
salt and black pepper

- Put the bell peppers, sweet potatoes, and onions in a large roasting pan with the thyme and garlic.

- Season well with salt and black pepper and drizzle with 2 tablespoons of the oil, then roast in a preheated oven, at 400°F, for 10 minutes.

- Meanwhile, heat the remaining oil in a skillet or ridged grill pan over medium heat and cook the chicken breasts for 4–5 minutes on each side, until golden.

- Remove the roasting pan from the oven, toss the vegetables, then nestle the chicken breasts among them and roast for another 15 minutes, or until the chicken is cooked through.

 Chicken and Red Pepper Salad
Whisk together 3 tablespoons olive oil, 1 tablespoon raspberry vinegar, ½ teaspoon Dijon mustard, 1 crushed garlic clove, and ½ teaspoon honey. In a large bowl, toss together 2 seeded and sliced red bell peppers, 1 thinly sliced small red onion, 12 halved green grapes, ¾ bunch of watercress, 4 cups each of arugula and spinach leaves, 3 sliced cooked chicken breasts, and 2 tablespoons toasted pumpkin seeds. Toss in the dressing and serve immediately.

 Chicken, Red Pepper, and Sweet Potato Soup Heat 1 tablespoon olive oil in a skillet over medium heat, add 2 diced red onions, 1 seeded and diced red bell pepper, and 2 crushed garlic cloves, and cook for 2–3 minutes, then stir in 3 peeled and diced sweet potatoes. Add 1 teaspoon ground cumin, then pour in 4 cups vegetable stock. Simmer for 15 minutes. Using a handheld blender, blend until smooth, then season with salt and black pepper. Shred 2 cooked chicken breasts and add the meat to the soup, then heat through for 1 minute. Serve with a swirl of plain yogurt.

QuickCook

Soups
and
Salads

Recipes listed by cooking time

30

2

10

10 Butternut Squash and Chickpea Soup with Hash Browns

Serves 4

4 cups prepared butternut
  squash soup
1 (15 oz) can chickpeas, drained
4 potatoes, peeled and grated
2 tablespoons butter
1 tablespoon olive oil
½ cup grated Manchego cheese

- Heat the butternut squash soup according to the package directions, stirring in the chickpeas halfway through the cooking time.

- Meanwhile, squeeze out any moisture from the grated potatoes, using a dish towel.

- Heat the butter and oil in a large skillet. Shape the potato into 4 rough patties and place in the pan. Cook for 3–4 minutes on one side, then turn over, sprinkle with the cheeese, and cook for another 3–4 minutes, until golden. Serve the hash browns with the soup.

---

20 Creamy Curried Chickpea and Butternut Squash Soup

Heat 1 tablespoon oil in a saucepan over medium heat, add 1 chopped onion, and cook for 1–2 minutes. Add 1 peeled Yukon gold potato, cut into chunks, 1 (15 oz) can of chickpeas, rinsed and drained, 1 butternut squash, peeled and cut into chunks, and 1 teaspoon mild curry powder, and mix well to coat the vegetables with the spice. Pour in 2½ cups vegetable stock and add ⅔ cup dry shredded coconut, then bring to a boil. Simmer for 12–15 minutes, stirring occasionally, until the potato and pumpkin are soft. Using a handheld blender, blend until smooth and creamy. Heat ½ tablespoon olive oil in a small skillet, add 1 teaspoon cumin seeds and 2 tablespoons pumpkins seeds, and stir-fry for 2–3 minutes, until they start browning. Serve the pumpkin soup in bowls topped with the spicy pumpkin seeds.

30 Butternut Squash and Chickpea Salad

Put ½ butternut squash, peeled and cut into chunks, and 1 red onion cut into wedges in a roasting pan and season. Sprinkle with 1 tablespoon olive oil and 2–3 thyme springs. Roast in a preheated oven, at 400°F, for 15–20 minutes, until tender. Meanwhile, soak ½ cup couscous in cold water for 10 minutes, then fluff it up with a fork. Mix in ¼ cup chopped pecans, 1 (15 oz) can chickpeas, rinsed and drained, and 1 teaspoon harissa paste. Gently mix the squash in with the couscous. Divide 2 cups arugula leaves among 4 bowls and spoon the couscous over the greens. Whisk together 1 tablespoon olive oil and 2 tablespoons lemon juice and drizzle over the top.

GLU-SOUP-HAI

2 🕐 Italian Bean and Truffle Soup

Serves 4

2 tablespoons olive oil
1 onion, chopped
2 garlic cloves, sliced
1 (15 oz) can cannellini beans,
  rinsed and drained
1 (15 oz) can lima beans, rinsed
  and drained
1 (14½ oz) can diced tomatoes
½ savoy cabbage, shredded
½ tablespoon chopped fresh
  rosemary
3½ cups vegetable stock
1 teaspoon truffle oil
salt and black pepper
¼ cup grated Parmesan cheese,
  to serve

- Heat the oil in a saucepan over medium heat, add the onion, and cook for 1–2 minutes, until softened.

- Stir the garlic, cannellini beans, and lima beans into the onions and cook for 1 minute.

- Add the tomatoes, cabbage, and rosemary to the pan, then pour in the stock and the truffle oil. Mix together well, season, and bring to a boil. Simmer for 10–12 minutes, until the cabbage is just cooked.

- Divide the soup among 4 shallow dishes and sprinkle with the Parmesan to serve.

 Italian Bean and Truffle Salad
Steam 1½ cups trimmed green beans for 2–3 minutes, then refresh under cold running water and toss together with 1 (15 oz) can each of cannellini beans and lima beans, rinsed and drained, 8 halved cherry tomatoes, 4 sliced scallions, and 2 tablespoons chopped parsley. Whisk together 3 tablespoons olive oil, 2 teaspoons truffle oil, 1 tablespoon balsamic vinegar, and 1 teaspoon honey, pour over the salad, and toss to serve.

Sweet Potato and Three-Bean Truffle Salad Cook 4 peeled and thickly sliced sweet potatoes in a large saucepan of boiling water for 5 minutes. Drain, then toss with 1 tablespoon olive oil. Heat a ridged grill pan until hot and cook the sweet potato slices, in batches, for 3–4 minutes on each side, until they are slightly caramelized at the edges. Meanwhile, cook 1½ cups trimmed green beans in boiling water for 2 minutes, then drain and refresh under cold running water. Mix the beans with

1 (15 oz) can of lima beans, rinsed and drained, 2 halved cherry tomatoes, 1 thinly sliced red onion, and ½ cucumber, chopped. Whisk together 3 tablespoons extra virgin olive oil, 1 teaspoon truffle oil, 1 teaspoon Dijon mustard, and 1 tablespoon balsamic vinegar. Toss the beans with the dressing and serve the bean salad spooned over the slices of grilled sweet potato.

 # Chilled Avocado Soup

Serves 4

4 large avocados, peeled
and pitted
juice of 1 lime
½ red chile, seeded and diced
4 cups vegetable stock, chilled
2 scallions, finely sliced
½ red bell pepper, seeded
and diced
¼ cucumber, diced
1 tablespoon cilantro leaves
2 tablespoons olive oil
2 teaspoons lemon juice
2 tablespoons pumpkin seeds,
toasted
salt and black pepper
8 ice cubes, to serve

- Put the avocados, lime juice, and chile in a food processor and blend with the chilled stock until smooth. Season to taste with salt and black pepper and chill for 15 minutes.

- Meanwhile, mix together the remaining ingredients.

- Place 2 ice cubes in each of 4 shallow bowls and pour the soup over them.

- Sprinkle with the salsa and serve.

 ### Guacamole Avocado Salad

Mix together 3 peeled, pitted, and chopped avocados, 2 diced tomatoes, 1 diced red chile, 2 crushed garlic cloves, 1 small bunch of cilantro, chopped, the juice of ½ lime, and some salt and black pepper, then lightly mash together. Toss 8 cups mixed salad greens and ½ sliced cucumber with 2 tablespoons of your favorite salad dressing. Divide the salad greens among 4 plates and top with the guacamole to serve.

 ### Warm Avocado Salad with Chorizo

Heat 2 tablespoons olive oil in a saucepan and sauté 3 thick slices of gluten-free bread, cut into ¾ inch cubes, until golden. Remove the croutons from the pan. Add 6 oz chorizo to the pan and cook for 3–4 minutes, until it starts releasing its oil, then add 16 cherry tomatoes. Cook for 2–3 minutes, then add 2 tablespoons balsamic vinegar and a pinch of superfine or granulated sugar. Toss together 6 cups mixed salad greens and 2 peeled, pitted, and sliced avocados with the croutons. Spoon the chorizo and tomatoes over the greens, then drizzle with the juices from the pan and serve immediately.

30 Salmon Soup

Serves 4

3½ cups cauliflower florets
4 tablespoons unsalted butter
1 onion, chopped
1 leek, shredded
5 Yukon gold or red-skinned
   potatoes, peeled and diced
2 cups peeled and diced rutabaga
5 cups fish stock
2 tomatoes, chopped
1 lb salmon fillet, cut into
   large chunks
½ cup heavy cream
1 teaspoon creamed horseradish
juice of ½ lemon
small bunch of dill, coarsely
   chopped
salt and black pepper

- Cook the cauliflower in a large saucepan of boiling water for 4–5 minutes, until tender. Drain and reserve.

- Meanwhile, melt the butter in a large saucepan over medium heat, add the onion and leek, and cook for 3–4 minutes.

- Add the potatoes and rutabaga to the pan and cook for another 2 minutes. Pour in the stock and bring to a boil. Cover and simmer for 10 minutes.

- Add the tomatoes and cauliflower and cook for another 4–5 minutes.

- Gently add the salmon to the soup and cook for 5 minutes, until the fish is just cooked.

- Add the cream, horseradish, and lemon juice and stir gently. Sprinkle in the dill and season to taste with salt and black pepper.

 Smoked Salmon Salad

Divide 8 cups mixed salad greens among 4 plates. Top with 4 sliced cooked fresh beets, ¼ sliced cucumber, 8 halved radishes, and 12 chopped cherry tomatoes, then add 12 oz strips of smoked salmon. Whisk 1 teaspoon creamed horseradish into 2 tablespoons of your favorite salad dressing and drizzle it over the salad. Sprinkle with 1 tablespoon toasted sesame seeds to serve.

 Broiled Salmon with Pan-Fried Dill Potatoes Cook 4 peeled and thickly sliced red-skinned or white round potatoes in a saucepan of boiling water for 10–12 minutes, then drain. Return to the pan and shake the pan to fluff up the edges of the potatoes. Heat 2 tablespoons olive oil in a skillet, add the potatoes, and cook for 8 minutes, turning regularly. Meanwhile, broil 4 (5 oz) salmon fillets under a preheated hot broiler for 3–4 minutes on each side, or until cooked to your preference. Mix 2 tablespoons creamed horseradish with ⅓ cup plain yogurt, then stir in ¼ grated cucumber. Toss the potatoes with 2 tablespoons chopped dill and season well with salt and black pepper. Serve the salmon on a bed of dill potatoes, with a dollop of the horseradish yogurt.

 # Leek and Arugula Soup

Serves 4

1 tablespoon olive oil,
   plus extra to serve
6 leeks, sliced
2 cups vegetable stock
2½ cups arugula leaves
½ cup crème fraîche
1 cup soy milk
salt and black pepper

- Heat the oil in a saucepan over medium heat, add the leeks, and cook for 8–10 minutes, until softening.

- Pour in the stock, add the arugula leaves, and simmer for 4–6 minutes.

- Add the crème fraîche and milk, then blend until smooth, using a handheld blender. Bring back to a simmer and season with salt and black pepper. Drizzle over a little olive oil to serve.

 Leek, Arugula, and Chicken Soup

Heat 1 (28 oz) can of leek and potato soup in a saucepan according to the directions on the label. Meanwhile, shred 2 cooked chicken breasts. Stir the chicken and 1 cup arugula leaves into the hot soup and top with a dollop of plain yogurt to serve.

 Individual Leek Frittatas with Arugula Salad Brush the cups of two 12-section muffin pans with a little olive oil. Heat 1 tablespoon olive oil in a skillet and cook 1 large leek, diced, for 4–5 minutes. Meanwhile, mix together 6 eggs, ¾ cup heavy cream, ⅓ cup grated Gruyère or Swiss cheese, and ⅓ cup grated Parmesan cheese. Stir in the leeks and season with salt and black pepper, then pour into the prepared muffin pans. Bake in a preheated oven, at 400°F, for 20 minutes, or until just set. Meanwhile, toss together 2 cups arugula leaves, 12 quartered cherry tomatoes, 2 peeled and shredded carrots, and 1 finely sliced red onion. Toss the salad with your favorite prepared dressing and serve with the frittatas.

Spicy Sweet Potato and Red Pepper Soup

Serves 4

2 tablespoons vegetable oil
1 red onion, chopped
1 red bell pepper, seeded
  and chopped
3 sweet potatoes, peeled
  and chopped
¼ teaspoon ground cumin
8 cherry tomatoes
5 cups vegetable stock
⅓ cup dry shredded coconut
salt and black pepper

To serve

plain yogurt
cilantro sprigs

- Heat the oil in a saucepan over medium heat, add the onion and bell pepper, and cook for 3–4 minutes. Stir in the sweet potatoes, cumin, and tomatoes, and cook for another 2–3 minutes.

- Pour in the stock, bring to a boil, and simmer for 12 minutes. Stir in the coconut and cook for another 2–3 minutes. Using a handheld blender, blend the soup until smooth.

- Season with salt and black pepper and serve topped with a dollop of plain yogurt and a sprig of cilantro.

 Sweet Potato Salad Heat 1 tablespoon olive oil in a skillet and cook 3 sweet potatoes, peeled and diced, with 2 seeded and chopped red bell peppers for 8–9 minutes, stirring from time to time, until softened. Meanwhile, toss together 5 cups baby spinach leaves with ¼ bunch of watercress, 2 chopped scallions, 16 halved cherry tomatoes, and 2–3 tablespoons prepared salad dressing. To serve, toss in the sweet potato and bell pepper and sprinkle with 3 tablespoons toasted pumpkin seeds.

 Warm Sweet Potato Wedges Salad Slice 5 sweet potatoes into wedges. In a large bowl, mix together 2 crushed garlic cloves, ¼ cup olive oil, 2 teaspoons chopped sage, 1 teaspoon paprika, and some salt and black pepper. Toss the potato in the herb and spice mixture, put into a roasting pan, and roast in a preheated oven, at 400°F, for 25 minutes. Serve the potato wedges tossed with 8 cups baby spinach leaves and 4 chopped scallions.

30 Smoked Haddock and Potato Chowder

Serves 4

1 tablespoon olive oil

1 onion, chopped

2 celery sticks, sliced

12 oz new potatoes, cut
into bite-size pieces

2½ cups vegetable stock

2½ cups milk

12 oz smoked haddock or other
smoked fish, such as cod or
mackerel, or fresh white fish,
such as cod or halibut, cut into
bite-size pieces

1 tablespoon freshly chopped
parsley, to serve

- Heat the oil in a large saucepan over medium heat, add the onion and celery, and sauté for 4–5 minutes, until soft.

- Add the potatoes and sauté for 2 minutes.

- Pour in the stock and bring to a boil, then simmer for 13–15 minutes, until the potatoes are tender.

- Pour in the milk and bring back to a boil. Add the fish and cook for 4–5 minutes.

- Serve sprinkled with the parsley.

 Smoked Haddock and Potato Salad
Put 4 (5 oz) smoked haddock or other smoked fish fillets into a large, shallow saucepan and cover with 1¼ cups milk. Bring to a boil, lower the heat, and simmer for 8–9 minutes, until the fish is cooked. Meanwhile, poach 4 eggs in a skillet of simmering water for 4–5 minutes. Stir 2 teaspoons creamed horseradish into 2 cups prepared potato salad and divide among 4 plates. Top each with a piece of fish and a poached egg. Sprinkle with 2 tablespoons chopped chives to serve.

 New Potato and Smoked Haddock Salad Cook 1 lb halved new potatoes in a saucepan of boiling water for 10–12 minutes, until tender, then drain. Heat 2 tablespoons olive oil in a skillet, add the potatoes, and cook for 5–6 minutes, turning frequently, until lightly golden. Meanwhile, poach 1¼ lb smoked haddock fillets in 1¼ cups milk for 8–9 minutes, drain, and break into large flakes. Whisk together 1 tablespoon whole-grain mustard, ⅓ cup extra virgin olive oil, 1 teaspoon honey, and 1 tablespoon white wine vinegar. Toss 4 cups salad greens, 4 sliced scallions, and 12 halved cherry tomatoes in the dressing, then add the potatoes and fish and combine gently to serve.

10 Pea and Ham Soup

Serves 4

1 tablespoon olive oil
2 shallots, diced
2⅔ cups frozen peas
1½ cups vegetable or
  chicken stock
⅔ cup heavy cream
1 cup shredded ham

To serve

2 tablespoons crème fraîche
small handful of watercress

- Heat the oil in a large saucepan, add the shallots, and cook for 2 minutes. Add the peas and stock and bring to a boil, then lower the heat and simmer for 2–3 minutes.

- Remove from the heat and pour in the cream. Using a handheld blender, blend the soup until smooth. Season to taste with salt and black pepper.

- Gently reheat the soup and stir in the shredded ham. Serve topped with a dollop of crème fraîche and some watercress.

2 Pea and Ham Frittata Salad

Heat 1 tablespoon olive oil in an ovenproof skillet over medium heat, add 4 chopped slices of unsmoked bacon and 2 diced shallots, and cook for 1–2 minutes. Remove with a slotted spoon and reserve. Whisk together 6 extra-large eggs, then add the bacon, ⅔ cup thawed frozen peas, 1 cup chopped ham, and 1 tablespoon chopped parsley. Pour the egg mixture into the skillet and cook over medium heat for 12–15 minutes, until the underneath is cooked. Sprinkle with ¾ cup shredded cheddar cheese, then place the frittata under a preheated hot broiler for 2–3 minutes, until the top is golden and bubbling. Meanwhile, toss 8 cups salad greens with your favorite dressing. To turn the frittata out of the skillet, place a plate on top and turn upside down. Cut into wedges and serve on a bed of salad.

3 Pea and Ham Rice Stir-Fry

Cook ¾ cup long-grain rice for 8–10 minutes, or according to the package directions. Lightly beat 3 eggs with 1 teaspoon each oyster sauce and soy sauce. Heat 1 tablespoon oil in a wok, add the eggs, and scramble lightly, then remove and reserve. Add another tablespoon of oil and stir-fry 4 chopped scallions for 1 minute, then add 2 cups chopped ham and 1 cup thawed frozen peas. Cook for 2–3 minutes, then remove from the pan. Add the rice to the pan, stir in 2–3 teaspoons each tamari soy sauce and oyster sauce, and cook for 2–3 minutes. Return the ham and pea mixture to the pan with the scrambled egg and stir-fry for 3–4 minutes.

1 Lima Bean, Tomato, and Feta Salad

Serves 4

1 (15 oz) can lima beans, rinsed and drained

18 cherry tomatoes, halved

½ cucumber, chopped

1¼ cups crumbled feta cheese

juice of 1 lemon

1 teaspoon dried red pepper flakes

2 tablespoons olive oil

⅓ bunch of watercress

2 teaspoons sunflower seeds

1 teaspoon pumpkin seeds

½ teaspoon sesame seeds

- Put the lima beans, cherry tomatoes, cucumber, and feta into a large bowl.

- In another bowl, whisk together the lemon juice, red pepper flakes, and oil to make a dressing.

- Divide the watercress among 4 plates or shallow bowls.

- Toast together the sunflower, pumpkin, and sesame seeds in a small saucepan over low heat until starting to turn golden.

- Pour the dressing over the lima bean mixture and combine well.

- Spoon the lima bean mixture over the watercress, then sprinkle with the toasted seeds to serve.

---

2 Lima Bean Soup with Crumbled Feta

Heat 1 tablespoon olive oil in a large saucepan, add 1 chopped onion and 2 sliced celery sticks, and cook for 2–3 minutes. Stir in 2 teaspoons ground cumin and cook for another 2 minutes. Pour in 2½ cups vegetable stock, 1 (15 oz) can lima beans, rinsed and drained, and 1 (14½ oz) can diced tomatoes. Season with salt and black pepper and simmer for 8 minutes. Add ⅔ cup fava beans, 1 tablespoon chopped cilantro leaves, and the juice of ½ lemon and cook for another 2–3 minutes. Sprinkle with 1 cup crumbled feta.

3 Lima Bean and Tomato Curry

Heat 1 tablespoon olive oil in a saucepan over medium heat, then add 1 chopped onion, 2 seeded and chopped red bell peppers, and 2 crushed garlic cloves and cook for 5–6 minutes. Stir in 1 teaspoon ground cumin and ½ teaspoon each of ground coriander, turmeric, and chili powder. Cook for 1–2 minutes. Stir in 4 diced tomatoes and 2 (15 oz) cans of lima beans, rinsed and drained. Mash a few of the lima beans, then cover the pan and simmer for 8–10 minutes. Stir in a peeled and grated 2 inch piece of fresh ginger root and a pinch of garam masala and cook for another 2–3 minutes. Stir in 2 tablespoons chopped cilantro. Serve with steamed long-grain rice.

 # Roasted Potato and Tomato Salad with Honeyed Goat Cheese

Serves 4

1 lb new potatoes, halved
2 tablespoons olive oil
4 vines of cherry tomatoes
(about 6 tomatoes each)
4 thick slices of goat cheese
2 teaspoons honey
1 tablespoon balsamic vinegar
4 cups baby spinach leaves
½ cup chopped walnuts
salt and black pepper

- Blanch the potatoes in large saucepan of boiling water for 3–4 minutes, then drain.

- Pour the oil into a roasting pan and place in a preheated oven, at 400°F, for 1–2 minutes. Add the potatoes to the hot pan, season well with salt and black peppe,r and roast for 15 minutes.

- Add the tomatoes to the pan and roasted for another 5 minutes.

- Meanwhile, put the goat cheese onto a baking sheet and pour ½ teaspoon honey over each slice. Cook under a preheated hot broiler for 6–8 minutes, until golden and bubbling.

- Divide the spinach leaves among 4 shallow bowls and spoon the potatoes and tomatoes over the greens. Pour the vinegar into the roasting pan and mix with the pan juices.

- Place the goat cheese on the salad, sprinkle with the chopped walnuts, and drizzle with the pan juices.

 Broiled Goat Cheese with Tomato Salsa Put 4 thick slices of goat cheese on a baking sheet and pour ½ teaspoon honey over each one. Cook under a preheated hot broiler for 6–8 minutes, until golden and bubbling. Meanwhile, dice 2 tomatoes, 1 small red onion, and 1 peeled and pitted avocado and mix together with 2 teaspoons red wine vinegar. Serve the goat cheese on baby spinach leaves with the salsa spooned over the top.

 Roasted Tomato Soup with Goat Cheese Put 6 large tomatoes, in a roasting pan with 1 large chopped onion, 1 garlic bulb, halved horizontally, 5 black peppercorns, 2–3 thyme sprigs, and 2 tablespoons olive oil. Roasted in a preheated oven, at 400°F, for 15 minutes. Remove the tomato stems, thyme stems, and black peppercorns, then squeeze out the garlic bulbs and put them into a blender or food processor with the remaining contents of the roasting pan, 2 (3½ oz) packages sun-dried tomatoes, and 2½ cups vegetable stock. Blend until smooth. Pour the soup into a saucepan to reheat and serve sprinkled with ⅔ cup crumbled goat cheese and a few thyme leaves.

Quick Watercress, Beet, and Orange Salad

Serves 4

½ bunch of watercress
1 cup arugula leaves
1 orange, segmented
4 cooked fresh beets,
  cut into wedges
½ cucumber, chopped
2 tablespoons walnuts
⅔ cup crumbled feta cheese
prepared salad dressing of choice,
  to serve

- In a large bowl, toss together the watercress, arugula, orange segments, beets, cucumber, and walnuts.

- Sprinkle with the feta cheese and drizzle with the salad dressing to serve.

Watercress and Orange Soup

Heat 1 tablespoon olive oil in a saucepan over medium heat, add 1 chopped onion, and cook for 2–3 minutes, until starting to soften. Add 1 large diced potato and 1 bunch of watercress and cook for 1–2 minutes, then pour in the juice of 1 orange and 4 cups vegetable stock. Simmer for 10–12 minutes, until the potato is cooked. Stir in the grated zest of 1 orange, then, using a handheld blender, blend the soup until smooth. Season to taste with salt and black pepper and serve with a swirl of cream.

Spiced Watercress, Beet, and Orange

Salad Put 2 raw beets, peeled and cut into chunks, into a roasting pan and sprinkle with ½ tablespoon olive oil and ½ teaspoon cumin seeds. Roast in a preheated oven, at 400°F, for 15–20 minutes, until tender. Toss together ½ bunch of watercress, 2 segmented oranges, and 1 large carrot, peeled and shredded. Divide the salad among 4 plates, then top with the beets and 4 oz sliced or crumbled goat cheese. Sprinkle with ¼ cup coarsely broken pecans. Whisk together 2 tablespoons extra virgin olive oil, 1 tablespoon lemon juice, 1 teaspoon honey, ½ teaspoon Dijon mustard, ½ teaspoon freshly chopped rosemary, and some black pepper, then pour the dressing over the salad.

30 Roasted Cauliflower and Cashew Nut Salad

Serves 4

1 large cauliflower, cut into florets
1 (15 oz) can chickpeas,
  rinsed and drained
1 teaspoon cumin seeds
1 teaspoon coriander seeds
½ teaspoon ground turmeric
½ teaspoon ground ginger
½ teaspoon garam masala
¼ cup olive oil
1 cup cashew nuts
⅔ cup plain yogurt
¼ cup lemon juice
½ teaspoon Dijon mustard
5 cups baby spinach leaves
salt and black pepper

- Put the cauliflower into a roasting pan with the chickpeas, spices, some salt and black pepper, and 2 tablespoons of the oil. Roast in a preheated oven, at 425°F, for 15 minutes, then toss in the cashew nuts and roasted for another 10 minutes.

- Meanwhile, whisk together the remaining oil, yogurt, lemon juice, and mustard to make a dressing.

- Put the spinach on a large serving plate and spoon the spiced cauliflower over the greens.

- Drizzle with the yogurt dressing and serve.

 Raw Cauliflower and Cashew Nut Salad Chop 1 large cauliflower into small florets, then put into a food processor and pulse once to break them down. Whisk together 1 teaspoon grated fresh ginger root, 1½ tablespoons sesame oil, ½ tablespoon soy sauce, 1 tablespoon white wine vinegar, and ½ crushed garlic clove. Mix ½ cup coarsely chopped cashew nuts, a bunch of coarsely chopped cilantro leaves, and ½ tablespoon sesame seeds into the cauliflower, toss with the dressing, and spoon over a large plate of salad greens.

 Cauliflower and Cashew Nut Soup Heat 1 tablespoon olive oil in a large saucepan over medium heat, add 1 chopped onion and 1 chopped leek, and cook for 2–3 minutes. Add ½ teaspoon curry powder, 1 large cauliflower, cut into florets, and 1 peeled and grated parsnip. Pour in 5 cups vegetable stock, bring to a boil, and then simmer for 10 minutes. Process ½ cup cashew nuts in a blender, then add 1 cup of the soup and blend again until smooth. Add this to the soup to thicken it, then bring it back to a simmer. Season with salt and black pepper and serve with a drizzle of light cream on top.

30 Chickpea, Tomato, and Red Pepper Salad

Serves 4

3 large red bell peppers, seeded
  and cut into quarters
6 plum tomatoes, halved
¼ cup olive oil
1 teaspoon cumin seeds
1 tablespoon lemon juice
½ teaspoon Dijon mustard
½ teaspoon honey
1 (15 oz) can chickpeas, drained
10–12 basil leaves, coarsely torn
4 cups baby spinach leaves
salt and black pepper

• Put the bell peppers and tomatoes in a roasting pan and toss with 1 tablespoon of the oil and the cumin seeds. Season with salt and black pepper and roast in a preheated oven, at 425°F, for 20 minutes.

• Whisk the remaining oil with the lemon juice, mustard, and honey to make a dressing.

• Remove the bell peppers from the oven and spoon into a bowl. Stir in the chickpeas, basil, and spinach, pour the dressing over the salad, and serve immediately.

 Chickpea, Tomato, and Red Pepper Soup Heat 1 tablespoon olive oil in a large saucepan over medium heat, add 1 seeded and chopped red bell pepper and 1 diced red onion, and cook for 1–2 minutes. Stir in 1 (15 oz) can of chickpeas, rinsed and drained, and 3 chopped plum tomatoes. Pour in 4 cups vegetable stock and season well. Simmer for 4–5 minutes. Using a handheld blender, blend until smooth and serve with a drizzle of olive oil.

 Spicy Chickpea, Red Pepper, and Feta Salad Halve and seed 3 red bell peppers and put onto a baking sheet. Cook under a preheated hot broiler for 8–10 minutes, until blackened. Transfer to a bowl, cover with plastic wrap, and let rest until cool enough to handle. Heat 1 tablespoon olive oil in a saucepan over medium heat, add 1 seeded and sliced red chile, 2 sliced garlic cloves, and 4 scallions, and cook for 2–3 minutes. Remove from the heat and stir in 1 (15 oz) can of chickpeas, rinsed and drained, 8 halved cherry tomatoes, and 4 cups baby spinach leaves. Whisk together 2 tablespoons extra virgin olive oil, 2 tablespoons lemon juice, and a pinch of paprika. Peel the blackened skin off the roasted peppers and cut into slices. Mix the roasted peppers into the chickpea salad with the dressing and serve sprinkled with 1 cup crumbled feta cheese.

30 Butternut Squash, Asparagus, and Prosciutto Salad

Serves 4

1 butternut squash, peeled,
   seeded, and cut into chunks
2 red onions, cut into wedges
2 tablespoons pumpkin seeds
1 tablespoon olive oil
1¼ cups asparagus tips
12 slices of prosciutto
2 tablespoons extra virgin olive oil
1 tablespoon balsamic vinegar
2 endive heads, leaves separated
salt and black pepper

- Place the butternut squash and onions in a roasting pan, sprinkle in the pumpkin seeds, and toss with the olive oil and some salt and black pepper.

- Roasted in a preheated oven, at 400°F, for 22 minutes, until starting to caramelize, then toss in the asparagus tips and roasted for another 5 minutes.

- Place the prosciutto under a preheated hot broiler for 4–5 minutes, until crisp.

- Whisk the extra virgin olive oil with the vinegar to make a dressing.

- Divide the endive leaves among 4 plates and top with the roasted vegetables and prosciutto.

- Drizzle with the dressing and serve.

---

10 Asparagus-Prosciutto Wraps with Butternut Squash Soup

Wrap 12 spears of asparagus in 12 slices of prosciutto and place on a baking sheet. Drizzle with 1 tablespoon olive oil and bake in a preheated oven, at 400°F, for 3–4 minutes. Meanwhile, heat 1 (28 oz) can of butternut squash soup according to the directions on the label. Serve the soup with the asparagus wraps on the side.

20 Butternut Squash Soup with Prosciutto

Heat 1 tablespoon olive oil in a saucepan over medium heat, add 2 chopped onions, 1 crushed garlic clove, and 1 seeded and diced red chile, and cook for 2–3 minutes. Add 1 peeled and chopped butternut squash and cook for another 2–3 minutes, then pour in 4 cups vegetable stock, bring to a boil, and simmer for 15 minutes, until the squash is tender. Meanwhile, broil 6 slices of prosciutto until crisp, then coarsely break up. Using a handheld blender, blend the soup until smooth. Serve with a swirl of crème fraîche and a sprinkling of prosciutto pieces.

GLU-SOUP-JIL

Salmon and Watercress Salad

Serves 4

3 tablespoons extra virgin olive oil

juice of 1 orange

½ teaspoon mustard

½ teaspoon superfine or
   granulated sugar

½ bunch of watercress

¼ cucumber, chopped

2 oranges, peeled and segmented

2 tablespoons toasted walnuts

1 avocado, peeled, pitted,
   and sliced

6 oz smoked salmon strips

4 gluten-free pita breads,
   toasted, to serve

- Whisk together the oil, orange juice, mustard, and sugar in a small bowl to make a dressing.

- In a large bowl, toss together the watercress, cucumber, oranges, walnuts, and avocado.

- Toss with the dressing and smoked salmon and serve with the toasted pita breads.

 Broiled Salmon with Potato and Watercress Salad Cook 1 lb new potatoes, halved if large, in a saucepan of boiling water for 15–16 minutes, until tender. Meanwhile, mix together 2 diced shallots, 1 tablespoon coarsely chopped capers, 3 tablespoons mayonnaise, 1 tablespoon creamed horseradish, and 1 tablespoon chopped chives in a large bowl. Place 4 (5 oz) salmon fillets under a preheated hot broiler and cook for 4–5 minutes on each side, or until cooked to your preference. Toast 2 tablespoons pumpkin seeds in a dry skillet for 1–2 minutes.

Drain the potatoes and toss in the mayonnaise mixture with 1 cup coarsely torn watercress. Serve the salmon with the potato and watercress salad, sprinkled with toasted pumpkin seeds.

Salmon, Watercress, and Potato Soup Heat 1 tablespoon olive oil in a large saucepan over medium heat, add 1 chopped onion, and cook for 3–4 minutes, then stir in 3 peeled and chopped Yukon gold potatoes. Pour in 5 cups vegetable stock and simmer for 18–20 minutes. Stir in 1 bunch of watercress and cook for 1–2 minutes, until it has wilted. Blend the soup, using a handheld blender, until smooth. Stir in 2 tablespoons crème fraîche and season. Bring back to a simmer, add 6 oz salmon fillet cut into chunks, and cook for 2–3 minutes, then serve.

20 Sesame Seared Tuna with Spicy Cilantro Salad

Serves 4

2 (5 oz) tuna steaks
¼ cup tamari soy sauce
2 teaspoons honey
1¾ inch piece of fresh ginger root, peeled and grated
½ cucumber, cut into matchsticks
3 carrots, peeled and cut into matchsticks
6 scallions, shredded
small handful of cilantro leaves
2–3 tablespoons sesame seeds
1½ tablespoons lime juice

- Put the tuna into a nonmetallic bowl with the soy sauce, honey, and ginger and let rest for 15 minutes, turning once.

- Meanwhile, mix together the cucumber, carrots, scallions, and cilantro.

- Roll the tuna in the sesame seeds. Heat a ridged grill pan until hot, then cook the tuna steaks for 2–3 minutes on each side (the inside should still be pink). Let rest for 2 minutes, then slice thinly and serve on the cucumber salad, sprinkled with lime juice.

 Cilantro-Spiced Tuna with Salad
Put 1 cup cilantro leaves, 3 garlic cloves, a ¾ inch piece of peeled and chopped fresh ginger root, and 1 tablespoon lemon juice in a small blender and blend. Gradually add ⅔ cup olive oil to make a thick smooth sauce. Pour the sauce over 4 (5 oz) tuna steaks. Heat a ridged grill pan until hot and cook the tuna steaks for 2–4 minutes, turning once (cook for longer if you do not like your tuna pink). Serve with a crisp green salad.

 Seared Tuna with Coriander-Roasted Tomato Salad In a small bowl, mix together 3 tablespoons olive oil, 3 tablespoons balsamic vinegar, and 1 tablespoon crushed coriander seeds. Put 12 oz cherry tomatoes on the vine in a roasting pan and pour the vinegar mixture over them. Roasted in a preheated oven, at 400°F, for 15 minutes. Meanwhile, heat a ridged grill pan and cook 4 (5 oz) tuna steaks for 2 minutes on each side (longer if you do not like your tuna pink). Serve the tuna with the balsamic tomatoes on a bed of arugula leaves, sprinkled with 2 tablespoons coarsely chopped cilantro leaves

 # Beef Carpaccio and Bean Salad

Serves 4

8 oz tenderloin steak

3 tablespoons extra virgin olive oil

1 teaspoon black pepper

1 tablespoon chopped
    thyme leaves

1 teaspoon Dijon mustard

½ tablespoon balsamic vinegar

½ teaspoon honey

1 cup trimmed green beans

1 (15 oz) can cannellini beans,
    rinsed and drained

1 oz Parmesan cheese shavings,
    to garnish

- Put the steak on a cutting board and rub with 1 tablespoon of the oil, the black pepper, and the thyme. Wrap in plastic wrap and put into the freezer for 20 minutes.

- Meanwhile, whisk together the remaining oil with the mustard, vinegar, and honey to make a dressing.

- Blanch the green beans for 2–3 minutes in boiling water, then refresh under cold running water. Toss the green beans and cannellini beans in the dressing and let stand at room temperature.

- Unwrap the steak, slice as thinly as possible, and arrange on a plate. Spoon the bean salad over the meat with all the dressing and garnish with shavings of Parmesan.

 Quick Beef Carpaccio and Bean Salad Whisk together 3 tablespoons olive oil, 1 tablespoon balsamic vinegar, and 1 teaspoon each of mustard, and honey. Blanch 1 cup trimmed green beans for 2–3 minutes in boiling water, then refresh under cold running water. Toss in the dressing with 1 (15 oz) can cannellini beans, rinsed and drained, and let stand at room temperature. Arrange 8 oz thinly sliced store-bought beef carpaccio on a plate, spoon the bean salad over the meat, and garnish with shavings of Parmesan.

 Nutty Beef and Bean Salad Rub 1 lb top sirloin steak with 1 tablespoon olive oil and sprinkle with 1 tablespoon black pepper. Cook the steak in 1 tablespoon olive oil in a skillet for 1–2 minutes on each side, then let rest. In a large bowl, toss together ¾ cup mâche, 2 chopped cooked beets, 4 sliced scallions, 1 (15 oz) can lima beans, rinsed and drained, 12 halved plum tomatoes, and 2 tablespoons toasted cashew nuts. Whisk together 3 tablespoons extra virgin olive oil, 1 tablespoon balsamic vinegar, 1 crushed garlic clove, 1 teaspoon packed dark brown sugar, and ½ teaspoon whole-grain mustard, then stir in 1 tablespoon coarsely chopped peanuts. Slice the steak and place on top of the salad, then drizzle with the dressing to serve.

Honey and Mustard Chicken Salad

Serves 4

3 tablespoons extra virgin olive oil
1 teaspoon honey
1 teaspoon Dijon mustard
1 teaspoon lemon juice
3 skinless chicken breasts
2 tablespoons pumpkin seeds
¼ bunch of watercress
1 cup arugula
1⅓ cups frozen peas, thawed
1 large avocado, peeled, pitted,
  and cut into slices

- In a small bowl, whisk together the olive oil, honey, mustard, and lemon juice to make a dressing.

- Place the chicken breasts on an aluminum foil-lined baking sheet. Cook under a preheated hot broiler for 5–6 minutes on each side, until cooked through.

- Meanwhile, heat a small skillet over medium heat, add the pumpkin seeds, and dry-roast until golden, stirring frequently.

- Toss together the watercress and arugula and divide among 4 plates.

- Slice the chicken diagonally and divide among the plates of salad greens. Sprinkle with the peas, avocado, and pumpkin seeds, pour the dressing over the salad, and serve immediately.

Chicken, Avocado, Watercress, and Mustard Sandwich Spread 4 slices of gluten-free bread with 1 teaspoon whole-grain mustard. Divide 1 cup torn watercress between the slices of bread, then top with 2 sliced honey-roasted chicken breasts and 1 large peeled, pitted, and sliced avocado. Top with another 4 slices of gluten-free bread to make 4 sandwiches.

Chicken Kebab Salad with Honey-Mustard Dressing In a large bowl, mix together ¼ cup honey, 3 tablespoons each sunflower oil and tamari soy sauce, and 2 crushed garlic cloves. Stir in 4 skinless, boneless chicken breasts cut into bite-size pieces and 2 seeded red bell peppers, cut into chunks. Let marinate for 10 minutes. Thread the chicken and red pepper onto 8 skewers, presoaked in water to prevent them from burning, and cook under a preheated hot broiler for 12–15 minutes, until the chicken is cooked through, turning once. Meanwhile, toss together ½ bunch of watercress and 1 cup arugula with 1 peeled, pitted, and sliced avocado. Whisk together 3 tablespoons olive oil and 1 tablespoon white wine vinegar, 1 teaspoon honey, and 1 teaspoon Dijon mustard and drizzle the dressing over the salad. Serve the kebabs on a bed of salad.

 # Peppered Steak and Red Onion Salad

Serves 4

2 red onions, cut into wedges
⅓ cup olive oil
1 teaspoon thyme leaves
1½ tablespoons balsamic vinegar
1 teaspoon whole-grain mustard
1 teaspoon honey
4 (5–6 oz) tenderloin steaks,
   at room temperature
2–3 tablespoons black pepper
8 cups mixed salad greens

- Put the onions into a roasting pan, sprinkle with 1 tablespoon of the oil and the thyme, and toss together. Roast in a preheated oven, at 425°F, for 15–18 minutes.

- Meanwhile, whisk together 3 tablespoons of the remaining oil with 1 tablespoon of the vinegar, the mustard, and honey to make a dressing.

- Dust the steaks with the black pepper on both sides.

- Heat a ridged grill pan until really hot and add the remaining olive oil. Cook the steaks for 2–3 minutes on each side, depending on how pink you prefer your steak. Let rest for 2–3 minutes.

- Remove the onions from the oven and sprinkle with the remaining vinegar.

- Toss the salad greens with the dressing and add the balsamic onions. Serve with the steaks.

 ### Steak and Red Onion Sandwich

Slice 4 gluten-free French sticks in half horizontally and toast each side. Cook 1 lb tenderloin steak on a hot ridged grill pan for 2–3 minutes each side, or until cooked to your preference. Spread the bottom half of each bread stick with 2 teaspoons whole-grain mustard and top with 1 cup arugula leaves. Slice the steak and place on the arugula along with a thinly sliced small red onion. Top with the remaining bread halves to make 4 sandwiches.

 ### Steak with Red Onion Marmalade and Mashed Potatoes with Arugula

Heat 1 tablespoon olive oil in a saucepan over medium heat, add 3 sliced red onions, and cook for 1–2 minutes. Stir in 2 tablespoons balsamic vinegar, 3 tablespoons packed dark brown sugar, and a drizzle of honey, then reduce the heat, cover with a piece of wax paper, and cook for 25 minutes, stirring from time to time. Meanwhile, cook 7 peeled russet or Yukon gold potatoes in a saucepan of boiling water until tender. Heat a ridged grill pan until hot, drizzle in a little olive oil, and cook 4 (5 oz) steaks for 2–3 minutes on each side, or until cooked to your preference. Let rest. Drain and mash the potatoes with 4 tablespoons butter and a handful of arugula leaves. Serve the steak with the mashed potatoes with arugula and the red onion marmalade.

30 Quinoa and Feta Salad with Roasted Vegetables

Serves 4

1 red bell pepper, seeded
and cut into chunks
1 yellow bell pepper, seeded
and cut into chunks
1 red onion, cut into wedges
2 zucchini, sliced
2 garlic cloves
¼ butternut squash, peeled
and cut into chunks
2 tablespoons olive oil
1¼ cups quinoa
1⅓ cups crumbled feta cheese
small handful of parsley,
coarsely chopped
salt and black pepper

- Put the bell peppers, onion, zucchini, garlic, and squash into a roasting pan and toss with the oil. Roasted in a preheated oven, at 400°F, for 26–28 minutes.

- Meanwhile, cook the quinoa in boiling water for 8–9 minutes, or according to the package directions. Drain and refresh under cold running water, then set aside.

- Remove the vegetables from the oven. Remove the garlic cloves, squeeze out the flesh, and return it to the vegetables. Season well with salt and black pepper.

- Stir the quinoa, feta, and parsley into the vegetables and serve.

 Quinoa, Feta, and Raw Vegetable Salad Cook ¼ cup quinoa in boiling water for 8–9 minutes, or according to the package directions. Meanwhile, in a large bowl, mix together 2 diced large tomatoes, ½ diced cucumber, small bunch each of parsley and mint, chopped, 1 diced small red onion, 1 cup shredded snow peas, and 1 seeded and diced red bell pepper. Drain and refresh the quinoa under cold running water, then stir into the salad ingredients with 2–3 tablespoons of prepared vinaigrette and ⅔ cup crumbled feta cheese.

 Quinoa and Vegetable Soup with Feta Cook ½ cup quinoa in boiling water for 8–9 minutes, or according to the package directions. Drain and refresh under cold running water. Meanwhile, heat 2 tablespoons olive oil in a saucepan over medium heat, add 1 diced onion, and cook for 2–3 minutes. Add 2 crushed garlic cloves and cook for another 2 minutes. Add 2 peeled and chopped carrots, 2 sliced celery sticks, 1 chopped zucchini, ⅔ cup peas, and 1 seeded and chopped red bell pepper and cook for another 2–3 minutes. Pour in 5 cups vegetable stock and simmer for 15 minutes. Stir in the cooked quinoa and 2 tablespoons chopped parsley. Serve in warm bowls with ⅔ cup crumbled feta cheese sprinkled over the top.

GLU-SOUP-RIT

QuickCook
Family
Dinners

Recipes listed by cooking time

30

20

10

10 Homemade Fish Sticks

Serves 4

3 tablespoons gluten-free
  flour blend
1 extra-large egg, beaten
⅔ cup gluten-free fresh
  bread crumbs
3 tablespoons cornmeal
1 lb cod fillet, cut into
  8 thick pieces
3 tablespoons sunflower oil
1⅓ cups frozen peas
2 tablespoons butter or olive oil
4 eggs

- Place the flour and the beaten egg in two separate shallow bowls, then mix together the bread crumbs and cornmeal in a third bowl.

- Gently toss the pieces of fish first in the flour, then in the egg, and finally in the bread crumb and cornmeal mixture to coat.

- Heat the sunflower oil in a skillet over medium heat and cook the fish sticks carefully for 5–6 minutes, turning occasionally, until golden.

- Meanwhile, cook the peas in boiling water for 2–3 minutes.

- Heat the butter or olive oil in another skillet and fry the eggs to your preference.

- Drain the peas and serve with the fish sticks and fried eggs.

20 Herbed Fish with Asparagus and Peas

Mix ½ cup gluten-free fresh bread crumbs with ¼ cup cornmeal, ¼ cup grated Parmesan, the grated zest of 1 lemon, and 1 tablespoon chopped parsley. Boil 1¼ cups peas for 2–3 minutes. Toss 12 asparagus spears in 1 tablespoon olive oil and cook in a hot ridged grill pan for 5–6 minutes, tossing regularly. Meanwhile, cook 4 (5 oz) cod fillets in 1 tablespoon oil for 2–3 minutes, then turn over, sprinkle with the crumb mixture, and cook for 1–2 minutes. Place under a hot broiler for 1–2 minutes, until golden. Toss the vegetables with 1 tablespoon chopped mint.

30 Roasted Fish with Mashed Potatoes and Peas

Cook 5 russet or Yukon gold potatoes, peeled and cut into chunks, in boiling water for 12–15 minutes, adding 1 cup frozen peas 2 minutes before the end of the cooking time. Meanwhile, heat 1 tablespoon olive oil in a saucepan over medium heat and cook 4 (5 oz) cod fillets, skin side down, for 2–3 minutes, until the skin is crisp. Place in a roasting pan and add 3 cups halved cherry tomatoes, ½ cup halved olives, and 3 tablespoons pine nuts. Season well with salt and black pepper. Roasted in a preheated oven, at 400°F, for 12–15 minutes, until the fish is tender. Drain the potatoes and peas and mash with 4 tablespoons butter and 1 tablespoon chopped mint. Remove the fish from the roasting pan and keep warm. Place the roasting pan on the stove over medium heat, stir in 2 tablespoons pesto and 2–3 tablespoons olive oil, and heat for 1–2 minutes. Place the fish on a bed of mashed potatoes, pour the pesto tomato sauce over the fish, and sprinkle with a few basil leaves to serve.

20 Roasted Pork Chops with Apple and Celery Salad

Serves 4

4 (6 oz) pork chops
1 tablespoon olive oil
1 teaspoon fennel seeds
2 tablespoons extra virgin olive oil
2 tablespoons red wine vinegar
2–3 sage leaves, chopped
4 sweet, crisp apples, cored and
 thinly sliced into rings
3 celery sticks, thickly sliced
12 green grapes, halved
black pepper

- Brush the chops with the olive oil and sprinkle with the fennel seeds and black pepper.

- Place on a rack over a roasting pan and bake in a preheated oven, at 400°F, for 20 minutes.

- Meanwhile, whisk together the extra virgin olive oil, vinegar, and sage to make a dressing.

- Toss the apples, celery, and grapes together with the dressing and serve with the roasted chops.

 Pork Cutlets with Caramelized Apples Melt 2 tablespoons butter in a skillet over medium heat, add 4 peeled, cored, and sliced sweet, crisp apples, and cook for 6–8 minutes. Mix together 4 teaspoons ketchup, 2 tablespoons packed dark brown sugar, 1 tablespoon white wine vinegar, and 1 teaspoon paprika. Heat 1 tablespoon olive oil in another skillet and cook 4 (5 oz) pork cutlets for 3–4 minutes on each side. Pour in the sauce and cook for another 1–2 minutes. Serve the pork cutlets with the apple and some steamed green vegetables, if desired.

 Rosemary Pork Chops with Roasted Potatoes and Apples Cook 5 russet potatoes, peeled and cut into chunks, in a large saucepan of boiling water for 12–15 minutes, until tender. Drain, return to the pan, and shake to rough up the edges of the potatoes. Meanwhile, heat 2 tablespoons olive oil and 2 tablespoons butter in a roasting pan in a preheated oven, at 400°F, for 5–6 minutes. Score the fat of 4 (6 oz) pork chops with a sharp knife and sprinkle with salt and black pepper. Heat a nonstick skillet and brown the pork chops for 2–3 minutes on each side, then add to the roasting pan with the potatoes, 2–3 sprigs rosemary, and 3 cored and chopped apples. Roasted for another 10–12 minutes, until the pork is cooked through and the potatoes are golden.

30 Chicken and Cashew Nut Curry

Serves 4

2 teaspoons cumin seeds

1 tablespoon coriander seeds

½ teaspoon fennel seeds

2 curry leaves

2 tablespoons sunflower oil

4 chicken breasts, chopped

1 onion, chopped

2 garlic cloves, crushed

½ inch piece of fresh ginger root,
  peeled and grated

1 red chile, seeded and diced

2 cups chicken stock

1 cup dry shredded coconut

1 (12 oz) package baby spinach
  leaves

½ cup cashew nuts, toasted

2 tablespoons chopped
  fresh cilantro

- Heat a small skillet over medium heat, add the spices and curry leaves, and dry-fry until they are fragrant. Grind in a mortar and pestle or grinder.

- Heat the oil in a saucepan over medium heat, add the chicken, and brown for 3– 4 minutes. Add the onion, garlic, ginger, chile, and ground spice mix and cook for another 3–4 minutes.

- Pour in the chicken stock and add the coconut, then bring to a boil. Simmer for 10–15 minutes, then stir in the spinach and cashew nuts. Season to taste with salt and black pepper.

- Sprinkle with the chopped cilantro and serve with basmati or other long-grain rice, if disired.

---

10 Chicken and Cashew Salad

Dry-fry 1 teaspoon cumin seeds, ½ teaspoon fennel seeds, and ½ cup cashew nuts for 3 minutes. Toss 1 coarsely torn Romaine lettuce, 1 cup arugula leaves, 1 small sliced red onion, and ½ cup cilantro leaves with the nuts and 3 sliced cooked chicken breasts. Whisk together 3 tablespoons olive oil, 1 tablespoon each mustard and balsamic vinegar, and ½ teaspoon honey and pour the dressing over the salad.

20 Chicken and Cashew Stir-Fry

Mix together 2 tablespoons cornstarch, ⅔ cup chicken stock, 3 tablespoons tamari soy sauce, ½ teaspoon ground ginger, and ½ teaspoon chili sauce. Heat 1 tablespoon vegetable oil in a wok over high heat and stir-fry 1 lb skinless, boneless chicken breasts, cut into strips, for about 5 minutes. Remove the chicken from the wok and set aside. Add 1 chopped onion, 1 seeded and chopped green bell pepper, 1 (8 oz) can water chestnuts, drained, and 1 cup cashew nuts to the pan and stir-fry for 5–6 minutes. Pour in the cornstarch mixture and bring to a boil, stirring continuously. Add the reserved chicken and stir until the sauce thickens and the chicken is heated through. Sprinkle with chopped scallions and serve with cooked long-grain rice.

30 Macaroni and Cheese with Leeks

Serves 4

8 oz gluten-free macaroni or
  other short pasta

3 leeks, thinly sliced

3 tablespoons butter

3 tablespoons gluten-free
  flour blend

1 cup milk

¼ cup shredded cheddar cheese

⅓ cup light cream

4 cherry tomatoes, halved

⅔ cup shredded Gruyère
  or Swiss cheese

salt and black pepper

- Cook the macaroni according to the package directions. Two minutes before the end of cooking time, add the leeks to the saucepan.

- Meanwhile, melt the butter in a small saucepan over medium heat and stir in the flour to make a roux. Gradually whisk in the milk and continue to cook and stir until the sauce thickens.

- Take the sauce off the heat and stir in the cheddar cheese and cream. Season with salt and black pepper.

- Drain the pasta and leeks and return to the pan. Pour in the sauce and mix well, then pour the macaroni mixture into an ovenproof dish.

- Top with the cherry tomatoes and Gruyère cheese, then place under a preheated hot broiler for 6–7 minutes, until golden and bubbling.

 Leek and Cheese Pizza

Toast 4 gluten-free pita breads for 2 minutes on each side. Meanwhile, heat 1 tablespoon olive oil and 2 tablespoons butter in a skillet, add 3 thinly sliced leeks, and cook for 4–5 minutes, until tender. Top each pita with the leeks and sprinkle with 12 chopped cherry tomatoes and 1¼ cups shredded Gruyère cheese. Place under a preheated hot broiler for 1–2 minutes, until golden and bubbling. Serve with a crisp green salad.

 Leek and Cheese Fusilli

Heat 1 tablespoon olive oil and 2 tablespoons butter in a skillet over medium heat. Cook 1 teaspoon dried red pepper flakes for 1–2 minutes, then add 3 sliced leeks and cook for 6–7 minutes. Meanwhile, cook 12 oz gluten-free fusilli according to the package directions. Stir 12 halved cherry tomatoes into the leeks. Drain the pasta and stir into the leeks. Pour into an ovenproof dish, top with ¾ cup shredded Gruyère, and place under a preheated hot broiler for 3–4 minutes, until golden and bubbling. Serve with a crisp green salad.

Salmon Stew with Mashed Potatoes

Serves 4

1 tablespoon olive oil
1 onion, chopped
2 garlic cloves, crushed
1 teaspoon ground cumin
½ teaspoon paprika
1 (14½ oz) can diced tomatoes
1 red bell pepper, seeded and
  chopped
1 cup fish stock
7 russet or Yukon gold potatoes,
  peeled and chopped
1 lb salmon fillets, cut into
  large chunks
4 oz raw, peeled jumbo shrimp
4 tablespoons unsalted butter
2 teaspoons creamed horseradish
small handful of chopped parsley
salt and black pepper

- Heat the oil in a large saucepan over medium heat, add the onion, garlic, cumin, and paprika, and cook for 3–4 minutes.

- Add the diced tomatoes, red bell pepper, and stock and bring to a simmer. Cook for 8–10 minutes.

- Meanwhile, cook the potatoes in boiling water for 12–15 minutes, until tender.

- Add the salmon and shrimp to the tomato mixture and cook for 4–5 minutes.

- Drain the potatoes and mash with the butter, horseradish, and some salt and black pepper.

- Divide the stew among 4 bowls, sprinkle with the parsley, and spoon the mashed potatoes on top.

 Pan-Fried Salmon with Grilled Sweet Potatoes Boil 3 peeled and thickly sliced sweet potatoes for 5 minutes, then drain and toss with 1–2 tablespoons olive oil. Cook the slices in a hot ridged grill pan for 2–3 minutes, until the edges start to caramelize. Meanwhile, pan-fry 4 (5 oz) salmon fillets in 1 tablespoon oil for 2–3 minutes on each side, until cooked to your preference. Serve with a salad.

 Salmon Fish Cakes Heat 1 tablespoon olive oil in a skillet over medium heat, add 4 thinly sliced scallions, and cook for 3–4 minutes, then put into a bowl. Place 7 oz salmon fillets and 10 oz cod fillets under a preheated hot broiler and cook for 3–4 minutes on each side. Flake the fish and mix with the scallions, 2½ cups prepared mashed potatoes, and 2 tablespoons chopped dill. With wet hands, shape the fish mixture into 8 round cakes. Dust with 1–2 tablespoons gluten-free flour blend. Heat another 2 tablespoons olive oil in the skillet and cook the fish cakes for 3–4 minutes on each side, until golden. Meanwhile, steam 1 (12 oz) package baby spinach leaves until wilted, and heat 1¼ cups prepared cheese sauce. Serve the fish cakes on a bed of spinach with a drizzle of cheese sauce.

10 Quick Roasted Pepper Pizza

Serves 4

4 gluten-free pita breads
¼ cup ketchup
4 roasted red and yellow peppers
  from a jar, drained and sliced
4 scallions, sliced
5 oz mozzarella cheese, sliced
small handful of arugula leaves.

- Toast the pita breads for 2 minutes on each side. Top each one with 1 tablespoon ketchup and the roasted peppers, scallions, and mozzarella.

- Place under a preheated hot broiler and cook for 4–6 minutes, until bubbling and golden. Serve topped with the arugula.

 ### Roasted Pepper Pasta

Place 2 seeded and halved red bell peppers and 2 seeded and halved yellow bell peppers under a preheated hot broiler and cook for 10–12 minutes, or until blackened. Place in a bowl, cover with plastic wrap, and let sit until cool enough to handle. Meanwhile, cook 12 oz gluten-free pasta for 9–12 minutes, or according to the package directions. Peel the skin off the roasted peppers and slice the flesh. Heat 1 tablespoon olive oil in a skillet, add 2 sliced garlic cloves, and cook for 1 minute, then add the roasted peppers. Cook for 1 minute, then place the mixture in a large bowl. Drain the pasta and add to the bowl with 4–5 torn basil leaves and a small handful of arugula leaves. Toss, sprinkle with grated Parmesan, and serve immediately.

 ### Cornmeal Roasted Pepper Pizza

Bring 4 cups water to a boil in a large saucepan. Slowly pour in 2 cups cornmeal polenta, stirring constantly. Add 1 teaspoon dried oregano, season, and continue to cook, stirring, for 8–10 minutes, until the cornmeal is thick. Divide in half, pour out onto 2 lightly oiled baking sheets, and spread into a circle about ½ inch thick. Bake in a preheated oven, at 400°F, for 12 minutes. Spread 1 (14½ oz) can diced tomatoes over the cornmeal crust, top with 2 cups roasted pepper strips and 10–12 coarsely torn basil leaves, then sprinkle with 8 oz sliced mozzarella. Bake for 12–15 minutes, until the cheese is golden and bubbling. Serve hot, cut into wedges.

 # Roasted Duck Breast with Plum Sauce

Serves 4

4 duck breasts
1 tablespoon olive oil
2 shallots, diced
6 ripe plums, pitted and
  cut into small wedges
⅓ cup firmly packed light
  brown sugar
2 sprigs thyme
2 star anise
½ cup red wine
2 cups beef stock
salt and black pepper
steamed green vegetables,
  to serve

- Score the skin of the duck breasts with a sharp knife and season well with salt and black pepper.

- Heat a nonstick, ovenproof saucepan over medium heat, add the duck, skin side down, and cook for 6–7 minutes.

- Meanwhile, heat the oil in a saucepan, add the shallots, and cook for 3–4 minutes. Add the plums and sugar and cook for another 2–3 minutes, until the sugar has dissolved.

- Turn the duck breasts over and add the thyme and star anise to the pan. Transfer to a preheated oven, at 350°F, and roasted for 10–12 minutes.

- Meanwhile, add the wine and stock to the plums and simmer for 12–15 minutes, stirring occasionally.

- Remove the duck breasts from the oven and let rest for 5 minutes, then cut each one into slices.

- Divide the vegetables among 4 warm plates. Place the duck on top, with the plum sauce spooned over the duck.

 Smoked Duck Breast and Plum Salad Toss together the seeds of 1 pomegranate, ¼ cup toasted slivered almonds, 2 plums, pitted and cut into thin wedges, the leaves of 1 small frisée lettuce, and 2 tablespoons chopped chives with a prepared salad dressing of your choice. Divide the salad among 4 plates. Cut 2 smoked duck breasts into slices and place on top of the salad.

 Duck Breast with Plum Sauce and Crushed Potatoes Cook 1¼ lb new potatoes in boiling water for 12–15 minutes, until tender, adding 1 cup trimmed and halved green beans 3 minutes from the end of cooking time. Meanwhile, make the plum sauce as above. Score the skin of 4 duck breasts and season with salt and black pepper. Heat a nonstick ovenproof skillet over medium heat, add the duck breasts, skin side down, and cook for 5 minutes, until golden. Turn over the duck breasts, transfer the pan to a preheated oven, at 375°F, and cook for another 3–4 minutes. Remove from the oven and let rest for 5 minutes, then slice. Drain the potatoes and beans and return to the pan with 2 tablespoons butter and 2 tablespoons chopped chives. Lightly crush the potatoes, then divide them among 4 warm plates. Top with the sliced duck and pour over the plum sauce to serve.

10 Tagliatelle with Dolcelatte and Walnut Sauce

Serves 4

12 oz gluten-free tagliatelle

1 cup light cream

2 cups crumbled dolcelatte, gorgonzola, or other blue cheese

1 cup walnut pieces, toasted

2 tablespoons shredded basil leaves

- Cook the pasta in a large saucepan of boiling water for 8–9 minutes, or according to the package directions.

- Meanwhile, put the light cream in a skillet with the blue cheese and place over medium-low heat. When the cheese is melted, stir in the walnuts.

- Drain the pasta and toss in the creamy cheese and walnut sauce.

- Serve in warm bowls, sprinkled with the shredded basil.

 20 Dolcelatte and Walnut Tortilla Pizza Wilt 1 (12 oz) package baby spinach leaves in a saucepan with 1 tablespoon olive oil. Heat 2 gluten-free tortillas according to the package directions. Place the tortillas on baking sheets and spread with ¾ cup canned diced tomatoes. Sprinkle with 2 cups crumbled dolcelatte or other blue cheese and 1 cup toasted walnut pieces. Toast under a preheated hot broiler for 3–4 minutes, until bubbling and golden.

 30 Dolcelatte and Tomato Pizza Heat 1 tablespoon olive oil in a saucepan, add 3 sliced garlic cloves and 1 chopped small onion, and cook for 3–4 minutes. Stir in 1 (14½ oz) can of diced tomatoes and 6–8 torn basil leaves and cook for another 3–4 minutes. Place 2 gluten-free pizza crusts on a baking sheet and spoon the tomato sauce over them, spreading it to the edges. Top with 1 cup coarsely chopped watercress and 4 sliced tomatoes. Thinly slice ½ red onion and sprinkle it over the tomatoes, then top with 2 cups crumbled dolcelatte or other blue cheese and 2 tablespoons pine nuts. Bake in a preheated oven, at 425°F, for 20–22 minutes, until golden and bubbling. Serve with a crisp green salad.

GLU-FAMI-QOU

20 Mackerel Curry

Serves 4

1 green chile, seeded and chopped
1 teaspoon ground coriander
½ teaspoon turmeric
4 garlic cloves
1 inch piece of fresh ginger root, peeled and sliced
1 teaspoon sunflower oil
1 tablespoon coconut oil
1 teaspoon cumin seeds
1 large onion, sliced
⅔ cup coconut milk
1 lb mackerel fillets, cut into 2 inch pieces
small handful of cilantro leaves, coarsely torn
salt and black pepper

- Put the chile, ground coriander, turmeric, garlic, ginger, and sunflower oil in a small blender and blend together to make a smooth paste.

- Heat the coconut oil in a wok or skillet over medium heat, add the spice paste and the cumin, and cook for 2–3 minutes.

- Add the onion to the pan and cook for 1–2 minutes, then pour in the coconut milk and 1 cup water. Bring to a boil, then simmer for 5 minutes. Season with salt and black pepper.

- Add the mackerel to the pan and cook for 6–8 minutes, until the fish is cooked, then stir in the cilantro leaves.

---

10 Mackerel and Orange Cumin Couscous Salad Cover 1½ cups couscous with boiling water and let stand for 8 minutes. Segment 2 oranges and break 4 smoked mackerel fillets into large flakes. Whisk together 3 tablespoons olive oil, ¼ cup lemon juice, 1 teaspoon each honey and Dijon mustard, and ½ teaspoon ground cumin. Fluff up the couscous with a fork and stir in the orange segments, fish, ½ chopped cucumber, 2 tablespoons chopped parsley, ¼ bunch of watercress, and the dressing.

30 Cumin Beets with Mackerel and Horseradish Cut 8 beets into 4–6 wedges, put into a roasting pan with 2 tablespoons olive oil, 2 teaspoons cumin seeds, 2 tablespoons thyme, and 2 teaspoons honey, and mix to coat. Roast in a preheated oven, at 400°F, for 25 minutes. Meanwhile, whisk together 2 tablespoons creamed horseradish, ¼ cup lemon juice, and ⅔ cup plain yogurt. Heat 4 smoked mackerel fillets according to the package directions and flake into large flakes. Place a few small handfuls of baby spinach leaves onto 4 plates and spread the mackerel and beets over the greens. Sprinkle with the horseradish dressing and serve.

30 Spiced Lamb Casserole

Serves 4

2 tablespoons olive oil
1 lb ground lamb
1 large onion, chopped
2 carrots, peeled and diced
2 garlic cloves, chopped
1 teaspoon ground cumin
½ teaspoon ground cinnamon
½ teaspoon allspice
1 cup lamb stock
¼ cup tomato paste
1 teaspoon dark brown sugar
5 sweet potatoes, peeled
  and chopped
2 tablespoons butter
1 tablespoon chopped
  cilantro leaves
salt and black pepper

- Heat the oil in a saucepan over medium heat, add the lamb, and brown for 3–4 minutes, then remove from the pan.

- Add the onion, carrots, and garlic to the pan and cook for 2–3 minutes, then stir in the spices. Return the lamb to the pan and stir to coat with the spices. Pour in the stock, stir in the tomato paste and sugar, and simmer for 12 minutes, stirring occasionally.

- Meanwhile, cook the sweet potatoes in a large saucepan of boiling water for 12–15 minutes, until tender. Drain and mash with the butter and salt and black pepper.

- Stir the chopped cilantro into the lamb, spoon into an ovenproof dish, and top with the mashed sweet potatoed.

- Bake in a preheated oven, at 400°F, for 10–12 minutes and serve.

 Spiced Lamb Kebabs

Mix 1 lb ground lamb with 2 tablespoons lemon juice. In a blender, blend together 1 tablespoon olive oil, 2 cups cilantro leaves, 2 seeded and chopped green chiles, 4 crushed garlic cloves, 1 teaspoon ground cumin, ½ teaspoon each ground coriander, turmeric, and garam masala, and 2 teaspoons grated fresh ginger root. Mix the paste into the lamb and squeeze the mixture onto 8 skewers. Brush each kebab with olive oil and broil for 2–3 minutes on each side, or until cooked through.

 Spiced Lamb Chops with Chickpea and Red Pepper Salad In a large bowl, mix together ¼ cup lemon juice, 2 teaspoons ground cumin, and 1 teaspoon paprika. Add 8 lamb loin chops, rub the spice mixture over the meat, and let marinate for 5 minutes. Heat a ridged grill pan and cook the lamb for 3–4 minutes on each side, then let rest for 5 minutes. Meanwhile, mix together 1 (15 oz) can chickpeas, rinsed and drained, and ⅔ cup sliced roasted red peppers in a bowl. Heat 2 tablespoons olive oil in a skillet, add 1 thinly sliced red onion, and cook for 2–3 minutes. Add 2 sliced garlic cloves and cook for another minute, then pour in 2 tablespoons red wine vinegar. Pour the onion mixture over the chickpea mixture and stir in with 2 tablespoons chopped cilantro leaves. Divide the salad among 4 plates and top each one with 2 lamb chops.

30 Mushroom Risotto

Serves 4

2 oz dried porcini

4 cups hot vegetable stock

1 tablespoon olive oil

4 tablespoons unsalted butter

1½ cups sliced cremini mushrooms

1 garlic clove, crushed

3 shallots, chopped

1½ cups risotto rice

⅓ cup white wine

1½ cups grated Parmesan cheese

- Put the dried porcini in a small bowl and cover with some of the stock. Let stand for 10 minutes. Keep the remaining stock warm over low heat.

- Heat the oil and butter in a saucepan over medium heat, add the mushrooms, garlic, and shallots, and cook for 2–3 minutes.

- Add the rice and stir until well coated, then pour in the wine and let it simmer until it has all been absorbed by the rice.

- Add a ladle of the hot stock to the pan and cook, stirring, until all the stock has been absorbed. Repeat this process until the rice is tender, but still has a slight bite.

- Remove the porcini from the stock and coarsely chop, then stir into the risotto with 1 cup of the grated Parmesan.

- Serve with the remaining Parmesan sprinkled over the top.

 Portobello Mushrooms with Mushroom Risotto Prepare 2 (8 oz) packages mushroom risotto according to the package directions. Meanwhile, put 4 portobello mushrooms on a baking sheet and sprinkle with 2 teaspoons chopped thyme leaves and 2 tablespoons olive oil. Place under a preheated broiler and cook for 8 minutes. Spoon the risotto into the mushrooms and sprinkle with 2 tablespoons grated Parmesan.

Mushrooms and Red Peppers with Rice Heat 1 tablespoon olive oil in a saucepan over medium heat, add 1 large chopped onion, 4 cups sliced white button mushrooms, 2 tablespoons chopped thyme, and 2 seeded and sliced red bell peppers, and cook for 3–4 minutes. Stir in 1 cup basmati or other long-grain rice, 1 (14½ oz) can diced tomatoes, 1¾ cups vegetable stock, and some salt and black pepper. Bring to a boil, then cover and simmer for 17–18 minutes, until the rice is cooked. Sprinkle with 2 tablespoons chopped parsley to serve.

10 Spaghetti Arrabiata with Chile and Shrimp

Serves 4

12 oz gluten-free spaghetti
3 tablespoons olive oil
½ red chile, diced
4 garlic cloves, crushed
8 ripe tomatoes, skinned
2 tablespoons lemon juice
½ teaspoon superfine or
  granulated sugar
8 oz jumbo shrimp, cooked
  and peeled
small handful of basil,
  coarsely torn
Parmesan cheese shavings,
  to serve

- Cook the spaghetti in a large saucepan of boiling water for 8–9 minutes, or according to the package directions, until "al dente."

- Meanwhile, heat the oil in a skillet over medium heat, add red chile and garlic, and cook for 1–2 minutes.

- Add the tomatoes, lemon juice, and sugar and cook for another 6–7 minutes, adding the shrimp for the last minute of cooking time.

- Drain the pasta and toss in the arrabiata sauce. Stir in the torn basil.

- Serve sprinkled with Parmesan shavings.

 2 Chile Shrimp Stir-Fry Cook 5 oz rice noodles according to the package directions. Drain and toss with 1 teaspoon sesame oil. Heat 2 teaspoons oil in a wok, stir-fry 2 seeded and diced red chiles, 2 teaspoons grated ginger root, and 3 crushed garlic cloves for 1 minute, then add 1 chopped red bell pepper, 1½ cups small broccoli florets, 4 sliced scallions, 12 cherry tomatoes, halved and 8 oz raw, peeled jumbo shrimp. Cook for 4–5 minutes, until the shrimp are pink, then add the noodles, 2 sliced bok choy, 1 tablespoon tamari soy sauce, and 2 tablespoons sweet chili sauce. Cook for another 3–4 minutes.

 3 Tomato and Chile Shrimp Pizza Put 3¼ cups gluten-free flour blend, ½ teaspoon salt, 2 tablespoons olive oil, 2¼ teaspoons active dry yeast and some salt and black pepper into a food processor and process until well mixed. With the machine running, gradually add a little water to make a soft dough. Transfer to a work surface and knead until the dough comes together. Divide into 4 and roll out each piece to a thin 10 inch circle. Place each one on a lightly oiled baking sheet. Mix together 1 (14½ oz) can diced tomatoes, 2 crushed garlic cloves, and ½ diced red chile. Spread the mixture over the pizza crusts and top with 8 oz cooked peeled jumbo shrimp, some torn basil leaves, and 8 oz sliced mozzarella. Bake in a preheated oven, at 425°F, for 12–15 minutes. Cut into wedges to serve.

30 Fish Casserole

Serves 4

1½ cups milk
4 oz salmon fillet, cut
  into bite-size pieces
12 oz cod fillet, cut into
  bite-size pieces
3 cups baby spinach leaves
2 eggs
8 oz raw, peeled jumbo shrimp
1½ tablespoons butter
1 tablespoon gluten-free
  flour blend
½ teaspoon mustard
4 sweet potatoes, peeled
  and chopped
½ cup shredded cheddar cheese
salt and black pepper

- Put the milk into a saucepan over medium heat and add the salmon and cod. Bring to a simmer and cook for 5–6 minutes. Drain the fish, reserving the milk.

- Put the spinach in an ovenproof dish and top with the fish.

- Boil the eggs for 3 minutes, until just softly boiled, then peel and cut into quarters and place on top of the fish. Sprinkle the shrimp around the dish.

- Melt the butter in a small saucepan over medium heat and stir in the flour to make a roux. Stir in the mustard, then gradually add the reserved milk, whisking continuously until you have a thick and creamy sauce. Pour it over the fish.

- Cook the sweet potatoes in a saucepan of boiling water for 12-15 minutes, until tender, then drain and mash with plenty of black pepper. Spoon the potato over the fish, then use a fork to spread it around in attractive patterns. Top with the cheddar cheese.

- Bake in a preheated oven, at 400°F, for 15–18 minutes.

---

1 Mashed Potatoes with Fish and Egg

Heat 2½ cups prepared mashed potatoes in a microwave. Broil 4 (5 oz) cod fillets on each side for 3–4 minutes, until cooked through. Poach 4 eggs. Stir 2 tablespoons chopped chives through the mashed potatoes and divide among 4 plates. Top each with a cod fillet and poached egg, then spoon 2 tablespoons prepared warmed cheese sauce on top.

2 Quick Fish Casserole

Place 12 oz salmon fillets and 8 oz cod fillets under a preheated broiler and cook for 4–5 minutes on each side, then cut into chunks and put into an ovenproof dish. Meanwhile, boil 3 eggs for 8–9 minutes. Refresh the hard-boiled eggs under cold running water, then peel, cut in half, and put into the ovenproof dish with the fish. Sprinkle with ⅔ cup frozen peas.

Mix together 2 tablespoons smooth mustard, 2 tablespoons chopped chives, and 1¼ cups plain yogurt, and pour the sauce over the fish. Top with 4 cups prepared mashed potatoes and sprinkle with ¾ cup shredded cheddar. Bake in a preheated oven, at 400°F, for 10 minutes.

30 Cheese Roulade with Spinach and Walnuts

Serves 4

2½ tablespoons unsalted butter
¼ cup gluten-free flour blend
1 cup milk
pinch of cayenne pepper
4 extra-large eggs, separated
2 teaspoons Dijon mustard
¾ cup shredded cheddar cheese
½ cup finely chopped walnuts
1 cup cream cheese
4 cups baby spinach leaves
3 finely sliced scallions
salt and black pepper

- Melt the butter in a small saucepan over medium heat. Grease a 13 x 9 inch jellyroll pan with a little of the melted butter, then line it with parchment paper.

- Stir the flour into the remaining melted butter to make a roux. Gradually whisk in the milk and continue to cook until the sauce comes to a boil and is thick and creamy. Remove from the heat, add the cayenne, and season. Stir in the egg yolks, mustard, cheddar, and ½ cup of the walnuts.

- In a large grease-free bowl, whisk the egg whites with a handheld electric mixer until stiff peaks form. Fold the egg whites into the cheese mixture and gently pour into the prepared pan. Bake in a preheated oven, at 400°F, for 10–12 minutes, until firm to the touch.

- Sprinkle the remaining walnuts onto a piece of parchment paper slightly larger than the pan. Turn the roulade out onto the paper, peel off the lining paper, and use the paper to gently roll it up. Cover with a damp cloth and let cool slightly.

- Unroll the roulade, spread with the cream cheese, and sprinkle with the spinach and scallions, then reroll. Serve warm or cold.

 Spinach and Walnut Salad

Dry-fry ¼ cup chopped walnuts for 2–3 minutes. Whisk together 3 tablespoons olive oil, 2 tablespoons lemon juice, and ½ teaspoon each honey and mustard. Toss 4 cups baby spinach with 4 sliced scallions, ½ chopped cucumber, 4 sliced tomatoes, and the nuts. Sprinkle with 1 cup crumbled goat cheese and drizzle with the dressing.

 Spinach and Walnut Pasta

Dry-fry ½ cup walnuts for 2–3 minutes, then put them into a food processor with 1 chopped garlic clove, ¼ cup grated Parmesan, 2 cups baby spinach leaves, and 2 tablespoons lemon juice. Process until everything is broken up. With the food processor running, gradually pour in ¼–⅓ cup extra virgin olive oil until the pesto is the consistency you want. Cook 12 oz gluten-free pasta in a large saucepan of boiling water for 10–12 minutes, or according to the package directions. Drain the pasta and toss with the pesto. Serve sprinkled with Parmesan shavings.

2⃝ Crab and Mussel Tagliatelle

Serves 4

2 tablespoons olive oil
1 onion, chopped
2 garlic cloves, crushed
1 (14½ oz) can diced tomatoes
⅔ cup white wine
1 red chile, seeded and diced
12 oz gluten-free tagliatelle
12 oz mussels, cleaned
8 oz crab meat (white and dark)
¼ cup lemon juice
small handful of parsley, chopped
salt and black pepper

- Heat the oil in a skillet over medium heat, add the onion and garlic, and cook for 3-4 minutes. Add the diced tomatoes, white wine, and chile, season with salt and black pepper, and simmer for 8–9 minutes.

- Cook the tagliatelle in a large saucepan of boiling water for 9–12 minutes, or according to the package directions.

- Meanwhile, add the mussels to the tomato sauce, cover, and cook for 4 minutes, until all the shells are open (discard any mussels that do not open).

- Drain the tagliatelle and stir into the tomato sauce with the crab meat, lemon juice, and parsley. Mix well and serve immediately.

 ### Crab and Smoked Mussel Quinoa

Salad Put ¾ cup quinoa in a saucepan with 2 cups water and cook over medium heat for 8–9 minutes, until all the water has been absorbed or the quinoa is cooked. Drain the quinoa and place in a bowl with 8 oz crab meat (white and dark), 8 oz smoked mussels, 1 tablespoon chopped parsley, ½ tablespoon chopped basil, 4 diced tomatoes, ½ diced cucumber, ¼ cup lemon juice, and 1 tablespoon extra virgin olive oil. Mix well and serve on a bed of salad greens.

 ### Baked Crab and Mussel Penne

Cook 10 oz gluten-free penne in a large saucepan of boiling water for 9–12 minutes, or according to the package directions. Meanwhile, heat 1 tablespoon olive oil in a saucepan over medium heat, add 1 thinly sliced leek, 1 peeled and finely diced carrot, 1 diced celery stick, and 2 crushed garlic cloves, and cook for 4–5 minutes, until softened. Stir in 2 (14½ oz) cans of diced tomatoes and 2 tablespoons shredded basil leaves and cook for 8–10 minutes. Stir in the cooked and drained pasta,

8 oz dark and white crab meat, and 4 oz shelled mussels. Pour into an ovenproof dish and sprinkle with 1 cup grated Emmental or Swiss cheese. Cook under a preheated broiler for 8–10 minutes, until golden and bubbling. Serve immediately.

30 Creamy Herb-Stuffed Chicken Breast

Serves 4

4 skinless chicken breasts
⅔ cup cream cheese
2 garlic cloves, crushed
½ tablespoon chopped parsley
½ tablespoon chopped chives
10 slices prosciutto
½ tablespoon vegetable oil, for oiling
2 leeks, finely sliced
1¼ cups fromage blanc or heavy cream
salt and black pepper
crisp green salad, to serve

- Using a sharp knife, make a slit in the side of each chicken breast to make a little pocket.

- Mix together the cream cheese, garlic, herbs, and some salt and black pepper.

- Lay 2 slices of the prosciutto on a cutting board and place one of the chicken breasts on top. Spoon one-quarter of the cream cheese mixture into the chicken breast, then wrap around the prosciutto to seal the pocket. Repeat with the remaining ham, cream cheese, and chicken to make 4 packages. Place in a roasting pan and bake in a preheated oven, at 400°F, for 25 minutes.

- Meanwhile, chop the remaining prosciutto and cook in a lightly oiled skillet over medium heat for 1–2 minutes. Add the leeks and sauté for 2–3 minutes, then stir in the fromage blanc and some salt and black pepper.

- Serve the chicken with a crisp green salad and the bacon and leek sauce.

 Herbed Chicken Pitas

Mix ⅔ cup cream cheese with 2 tablespoons chopped fresh herbs of your choice. Toast 4 gluten-free pita breads for 2–3 minutes on each side, then cut along the long side to open like a pocket. Spread the inside of each pita bread with cream cheese. Slice 3 cooked chicken breasts, then stuff each pita bread with one-quarter of the chicken, 1¼ cups crisp salad greens, and a dollop of mango sauce.

 Lemon Chicken with Herb Quinoa

Cook 1 cup quinoa in 2 cups of boiling water for 9–10 minutes, or according to the package directions. Meanwhile, drizzle ¼ cup lemon juice over 4 chicken breasts, season with salt and black pepper, then cook on a hot ridged grill pan for 5–7 minutes on each side, until cooked through. Drain the quinoa and stir in 2 tablespoons chopped parsley, 1 tablespoon chopped chives, ½ tablespoon chopped mint, and 2 diced tomatoes.

Serve the chicken on a bed of the herb quinoa.

Mint-Crusted Rack of Lamb with Mashed Potatoes and Peas

Serves 4

1½ lb new potatoes, halved if large
1 cup peas, frozen or fresh
1 tablespoon olive oil
2 French-trimmed racks of lamb
2 cups gluten-free bread crumbs
2 tablespoons freshly chopped mint
2 tablespoons Dijon mustard
2 tablespoons butter
1 tablespoon crème fraîche
salt and black pepper
red currant jelly, to serve

- Cook the potatoes in boiling water for 12–15 minutes, until tender. Meanwhile, cook the peas in boiling water for 3 minutes, until tender.

- Heat 1 tablespoon of the oil in a skillet over medium heat, add the lamb, and brown on all sides for 2–3 minutes. Remove the lamb from the pan and place on a baking sheet.

- Mix together the bread crumbs and mint and season with salt and black pepper.

- Spread the fat side of each rack with the mustard and then press on the bread crumb mixture. Sprinkle with the remaining oil and bake in a preheated oven, at 400°F, for 12–15 minutes, until golden (or longer if you prefer your lamb less pink).

- Drain the potatoes and peas, then mash with the butter and crème fraîche. Season well with salt and black pepper.

- Remove the lamb from the oven and cut each rack in half.

- Divide the mashed potatoes among 4 warm plates and top with the lamb. Serve with red currant jelly.

 Lamb, Pea, and Mint Salad Broil 8 lamb cutlets for 3–4 minutes on each side. Meanwhile, toss together 1 cup peas, 2 cups sugarsnap peas, 1½ cups pea shoots, 1 cup crumbled feta cheese, and a small handful of mint leaves. Whisk together 3 tablespoons olive oil with 1 tablespoon white wine vinegar and ½ teaspoon each Dijon mustard and honey. Drizzle over the salad and serve with the lamb.

 Pea and Mint Risotto with Lamb Chops Heat 4 cups vegetable stock. Meanwhile, melt 4 tablespoons butter in a heavy saucepan, add 4 sliced scallions, and cook for 2–3 minutes, then stir in 1 cup risotto rice. Pour in ½ cup white wine and cook, stirring, until it has been absorbed. Add a ladle of the stock and cook, stirring, until it has been absorbed. Repeat this step until the rice is tender but with a slight bite. Meanwhile, cook 1 cup frozen peas in boiling water for 3 minutes, then drain and lightly crush with 2 tablespoons chopped mint. Broil 4 lamb chops for 4–5 minutes on each side. When the risotto is cooked, stir in the minted peas and 2 tablespoons grated Parmesan. Season with salt and black pepper. Serve the lamb chops on a bed of risotto, sprinkled with 2 tablespoons of toasted pine nuts.

GLU-FAMI-NUZ

30 Pasta with Pesto and Roasted Vegetables

Serves 4

1 red bell pepper, seeded and chopped
1 yellow bell pepper, seeded and chopped
1 red onion, cut into wedges
2 zucchini, sliced
2 carrots, peeled and sliced
2 garlic cloves, sliced
8 cherry tomatoes
2 tablespoons olive oil
2 teaspoons cumin seeds
8 oz gluten-free pasta shapes
¾ cup pitted black ripe olives
2 tablespoons pesto sauce
small handful of basil leaves, torn
salt and black pepper
Parmesan cheese shavings, to serve

- Put all the vegetables, garlic, and tomatoes in a large roasting pan and sprinkle with the oil, cumin seeds, and some salt and black pepper. Roasted in a preheated oven, at 400°F, for 26–28 minutes.

- Halfway through the cooking time, bring a large saucepan of water to a boil and cook the pasta for 9–12 minutes, or according to the package directions, until "al dente."

- Drain the pasta and toss in the roasted vegetables, olives, pesto sauce, and basil leaves.

- Serve sprinkled with Parmesan shavings.

---

10 Pasta and Vegetable Salad

Cook 12 oz gluten-free pasta in boiling water for 8–9 minutes. Meanwhile, in another saucepan of boiling water, blanch 2 cups sugarsnap peas, 1 cup trimmed green beans, and 1 cup peas for 3 minutes. Drain and refresh under cold running water. Drain the pasta, then toss with the vegetables, 2 tablespoons pesto sauce, 1 cup crumbled feta cheese, 1 cup arugula leaves, and 2 tablespoons toasted pine nuts.

20 Roasted Vegetable Quick Pizza

Heat 1 tablespoon olive oil in a skillet over medium heat, add 1 seeded and chopped red bell pepper, 1 seeded and chopped yellow bell pepper, 2 thickly sliced red onions, 2 sliced garlic cloves, and 2 sliced zucchini, and cook for 10–12 minutes, stirring occasionally. Toast 4 gluten-free pita breads and spread with 2 tablespoons pesto sauce. Spoon the cooked vegetables over the pitas and top with 8 oz sliced mozzarella. Cook under a preheated hot broiler for 4–5 minutes, until the cheese is melted and bubbling.

30 Mediterranean Olive Chicken

Serves 4

4 (5 oz) chicken breasts
½ teaspoon paprika
1 tablespoon olive oil
1 red bell pepper, seeded
   and chopped
1 red onion, chopped
1 garlic clove, crushed
1 (14½ oz) can diced tomatoes
⅔ cup frozen spinach, defrosted
2 tablespoons green olives
1 teaspoon capers
1 tablespoon chopped basil

- Dust the chicken breasts with the paprika and cook in a hot ridged grill pan for 4–5 minutes on each side, then put into an ovenproof dish.

- Meanwhile, heat the oil in a saucepan over medium heat, add the bell pepper, onion, and garlic, and cook for 3–4 minutes. Add the diced tomatoes, spinach, olives, capers, and basil and bring to a simmer. Season to taste with salt and black pepper.

- Pour the sauce over the chicken and bake in a preheated oven, at 400°F, for 15–18 minutes, until the chicken is cooked through.

 Mediterranean Chicken Olive Pitas Toast 4 gluten-free pita breads for 2–3 minutes on each side, then cut along the long side to open like a pocket. Slice 3 cooked chicken breasts. Stuff each pita with one-quarter of the chicken, a small handful of baby spinach leaves, 3–4 halved olives, and 2–3 teaspoons tomato salsa.

 Chicken Kebabs with Tomato and Olive Salsa Cut 4 (5 oz) skinless, boneless chicken breasts into bite-size pieces and toss in a bowl with the grated zest of 1 lemon, 1 tablespoon chopped basil, and 1 crushed garlic clove. Thread onto 8 skewers, presoaked in water to prevent them from burning, with 1 seeded and chopped red bell pepper and 1 seeded and chopped yellow bell pepper. Cook under a preheated hot broiler for 15–16 minutes, turning occasionally. Meanwhile, mix together 6 diced ripe tomatoes, 1 diced shallot, 6–8 pitted and diced olives, 1 teaspoon lemon juice, 2 tablespoons olive oil, and 1 tablespoon shredded basil. Serve the cooked kebabs with the salsa.

30 Spicy Lamb Stew

Serves 4

2 tablespoons olive oil

1½ lb shoulder of lamb,
    cut into cubes

1 onion, chopped

1 garlic clove, crushed

1 teaspoon ground cumin

1 teaspoon ground cinnamon

½ teaspoon ground ginger

2 cups chicken stock

2 tablespoons tomato paste

1 teaspoon dark brown sugar

⅔ cup dried apricots

6 prunes

½ cup slivered almonds, toasted

cooked quinoa, to serve

- Heat the oil in a large casserole or Dutch oven over medium heat and brown the meat (you may have to do this in batches), then remove with a slotted spoon and set aside.

- Add the onion and garlic to the pan and cook for 2–3 minutes, then stir in the spices and cook for another minute.

- Return the lamb to the pan with the stock, tomato paste, sugar, and dried fruit. Bring to a boil, then simmer for 25 minutes.

- Serve sprinkled with toasted slivered almonds, along with cooked quinoa.

 Spiced Lamb Chops with Quinoa Salad

Cook ⅔ cup quinoa in boiling water for 8–9 minutes. Mix 2 teaspoons each turmeric, ground cumin, and ground cinnamon with 1 teaspoon ground ginger. Rub the spice mix over 4 (5 oz) lamb chops, then cook on a hot ridged grill pan for 3–4 minutes on each side. Meanwhile, mix together 2 tablespoons chopped parsley, 1 tablespoon chopped mint, ⅓ cup chopped dried apricots, and 2 tablespoons toasted slivered almonds. Drain the quinoa, stir in the herb mixture, and serve with the lamb chops.

 Spiced Lamb Burgers

Mix together 1 small diced onion, 1 tablespoon grated fresh ginger root, 3 crushed garlic cloves, ½ cup chopped cilantro leaves, 1 seeded and diced red chile, 1 egg, ½ teaspoon ground cumin, some salt and black pepper, and 1 lb ground lamb. Shape the mixture into 4 patties and chill for 6–8 minutes. Meanwhile, make the quinoa salad as in the recipe left. Heat 1 tablespoon olive oil in a skillet and cook the patties for 4–5 minutes on each side. Serve with the quinoa salad, a dollop of plain yogurt, and a sprinkling of paprika.

10 Pan-Fried Red Snapper and Mashed Potatoes with Fennel

Serves 4

5 peeled and diced russet or
 Yukon gold potatoes
2 fennel bulbs, trimmed and diced
1 tablespoon olive oil
8 (4 oz) red snapper fillets
2 tablespoons butter
1 tablespoon chopped parsley
watercress sprigs, to serve

- Cook the potatoes and fennel in a saucepan of boiling water for 8–9 minutes, until tender.

- Meanwhile, heat the oil in a saucepan over medium heat, add the red snapper fillets, and cook for 2–3 minutes on each side.

- Drain the potatoes and fennel and coarsely mash with the butter and chopped parsley. Serve the red snapper on a bed of the mashed potatoes with a few watercress sprigs.

2 Marinated Red Snapper with Leeks

Cut 3 slices into each side of 4 whole red snapper. Sprinkle with 2 tablespoons olive oil, 3 tablespoons lime juice, and 1 tablespoon fennel seeds, and let marinate for 10 minutes. Meanwhile, heat 1 tablespoon olive oil in a skillet over medium heat, add 3 sliced leeks, and cook for 5–6 minutes, until softened. Stir in 3 skinned and diced tomatoes and simmer for 4–5 minutes. Let cool for a few minutes. Spoon the leek mixture into the cavity of the fish. Cook under a preheated medium broiler for 7–8 minutes on each side, until cooked through. Serve with green vegetables and mashed potatoes.

3 Steamed Red Snapper and Mashed Potatoes with Fennel

Cut 8 pieces of parchment paper into squares large enough to cover a red snapper fillet, plus a 1½ inch border. Lightly brush 4 of the squares with a little oil and place on a baking sheet. Divide 1 (12 oz) package baby spinach leaves and 2 sliced leeks among the 4 oiled squares, then add 1 tablespoon crème fraîche, a splash of white wine, 2 red snapper fillets, 2 slices of lime, and some salt and black pepper to each one. Top with the remaining squares of parchment paper and fold up the edges to form packages. Bake in a preheated oven, at 400°F, for 15–20 minutes. Meanwhile, cook 2 trimmed and chopped fennel bulbs and 5 peeled and diced russet or Yukon gold potatoes in a saucepan of boiling water until tender. Drain and mash. Stir in 2 tablespoons butter and 1 tablespoon chopped parsley. Serve the fish and vegetables over a bed of mashed potatoes with fennel.

30 Ratatouille Pizza

Serves 4

2 x 1 (15 oz) cans ratatouille
2 crushed garlic cloves
¼ cup tomato paste
6–8 basil leaves, coarsely torn
4 gluten-free pizza crusts
1 cup grated mozzarella cheese
drizzle of olive oil
salt and black pepper

- Mix together the ratatouille, garlic, tomato paste, and basil leaves and season with salt and black pepper.

- Place the pizza crusts on 2 baking sheets, then spoon the ratatouille mixture over them.

- Sprinkle with the grated mozzarella, drizzle with the oil, and bake in a preheated oven, at 425°F, for 25 minutes, until hot and bubbling.

 Ratatouille Pasta Cook 12 oz gluten-free pasta in a saucepan of boiling water according to the package directions, until "al dente." Meanwhile, heat 1 (15 oz) can of ratatouille in a saucepan with 2 crushed garlic cloves, 6–8 torn basil leaves, and a drizzle of olive oil. Drain the pasta and toss in the ratatouille. Serve sprinkled with 2–3 tablespoons grated Parmesan.

 Ratatouille Pita Pizza Heat 1 tablespoon olive oil in a saucepan over medium heat, add 1 chopped red onion, 2 chopped garlic cloves, 1 seeded and chopped red bell pepper, 1 seeded and chopped yellow bell pepper, and 2 sliced zucchini and cook for 3–4 minutes. Stir in 1 (14½ oz) can of diced tomatoes, 6–8 coarsely torn basil leaves, and some salt and black pepper. Broil 4 gluten-free pita breads for 2 minutes on each side. Place the pitas on a baking sheet and spoon the ratatouille over them. Top with 1½ cups grated mozzarella and cook under the hot broiler for 3–4 minutes, until the cheese is golden and bubbling.

Thai Chicken Meatballs with Noodles

Serves 4

1 lb ground chicken

3 scallions, finely diced

2 garlic cloves, finely diced

1 red chile, seeded and
   finely diced

2 inch piece of fresh ginger root,
   peeled and finely diced

2½ cups chicken stock

12 oz rice noodles

1 cup prepared tomato sauce,
   heated

cilantro leaves, to garnish

- Mix together the ground chicken, scallions, garlic, chile, and ginger. Using wet hands, divide the chicken mixture into 16 portions and roll into balls.

- Pour the stock into a large saucepan and bring to a boil. Add the meatballs and simmer for 10 minutes.

- Meanwhile, cook the rice noodles according to the package directions, then drain and serve with the meatballs and tomato sauce, garnished with the cilantro leaves.

 Thai Stir-Fry Chicken with Noodles Cook 12 oz rice noodles in a saucepan of boiling water for 8–10 minutes, or according to the package directions. Meanwhile, toss 1 lb chicken breast strips with 2 tablespoons sesame oil, 1 seeded and diced red chile, 2 tablespoons peeled and grated fresh ginger root, and 3 chopped scallions. Heat 1 tablespoon vegetable oil in a wok, add the chicken, and stir-fry for 3–4 minutes. Add 2 tablespoons red Thai curry paste and stir-fry for another 2 minutes, then add 2 chopped bok choy and 1¼ cups coconut milk and bring to a boil. Simmer for 2–3 minutes. Drain the noodles, divide among 4 bowls, and spoon the chicken on top.

 Thai Chicken Curry with Noodles Heat 1 tablespoon vegetable oil in a wok over high heat, add 2 diced shallots and 1 diced lemon grass stalk, and cook for 1–2 minutes. Stir in 3–4 teaspoons red Thai curry paste and cook for 1 minute, stirring. Add 1¼ lb chicken breasts cut into bite-size pieces and stir-fry for 5–6 minutes. Add ½ tablespoon Thai fish sauce, 1 teaspoon brown sugar and a couple of kaffir lime leaves with 1¾ cups coconut milk. Bring to a simmer and cook for 15 minutes. Cook 5 oz rice noodles according to the package directions. Stir a small handful of coarsely torn cilantro leaves into the curry and serve with the rice noodles.

Seafood Stir-Fry

Serves 4

2 teaspoons honey
grated zest and juice of 1 lime
2 tablespoons tamari soy sauce
24 raw, peeled jumbo shrimp
2 oz squid rings
4 oz mussels, shelled
5 oz ribbon rice noodles
1 tablespoon vegetable oil
1 teaspoon sesame oil
4 scallions, sliced
1 red bell pepper, seeded
   and sliced
1½ cups bean sprouts
2 cups chopped bok choy

- Mix together the honey, lime zest, lime juice, and tamari. Put the shrimp, squid, and mussels into a bowl, pour over the marinade, and let stand for 5 minutes.

- Meanwhile, cook the rice noodles according to the package directions.

- Heat the oils in a wok over high heat, add the drained seafood, and stir-fry for 2–3 minutes, until the shrimp have turned pink. Remove and set aside.

- Add the scallions and red bell pepper and stir-fry for 2 minutes, then add the bean sprouts and bok choy and stir-fry for another 1–2 minutes. Return the seafood to the pan with the drained rice noodles and stir-fry for 2–3 minutes. Serve immediately.

Seafood Salad

Heat 1 tablespoon olive oil in a skillet over medium heat, add 1 crushed garlic clove, ½ seeded and diced red chile, and 1 (1 lb) package mixed seafood and cook for 4–5 minutes. Remove from the heat and remove the seafood from the pan with a slotted spoon. Stir 3 tablespoons lime juice and 2 tablespoons extra virgin olive oil into the pan. Toss the seafood with 4 cups arugula leaves and the dressing to serve.

Seafood Soup

Heat 1 tablespoon olive oil in a saucepan over medium heat, add 4 sliced scallions, 1 sliced celery stick, 1 seeded and diced red chile, and 2 sliced garlic cloves, and cook for 3–4 minutes. Pour in 1 (14½ oz) can of diced tomatoes and 2½ cups fish stock and bring to a simmer, then cook for 10–12 minutes. Stir in 1 (1 lb) package mixed seafood or fish and cook for 4–5 minutes. Serve sprinkled with 2 tablespoons chopped parsley and with toasted gluten-free bread on the side.

3⦿ Sausage and Onion with Mustard Mashed Potatoes

Serves 4

8 gluten-free sausages

4 red onions, cut into wedges

2 leeks, thickly sliced

3–4 rosemary sprigs

2 tablespoons olive oil

7 russet or Yukon gold potatoes, peeled and cut into chunks

4 tablespoons butter

2–3 tablespoons whole-grain mustard

black pepper

- Put the sausages, onions, and leeks into a large roasting pan, toss with the rosemary and oil, and season with black pepper. Roasted in a preheated oven, at 400°F, for 25 minutes, tossing a couple of times during the cooking time.

- Meanwhile, cook the potatoes in a saucepan of boiling water for 12–15 minutes, until tender.

- Drain the potatoes, return to the pan, and mash with the butter until smooth. Stir in the whole-grain mustard.

- Divide the mustard mashed potatoes among 4 warm, shallow bowls. Spoon the sausages, roasted vegetables, and any juices from the roasting pan over the potatoes.

 Quick Sausage, Onion, and Mashed Potatoes Heat 1 tablespoon olive oil in a large skillet, add 8 gluten-free sausages, and cook for 10 minutes, turning regularly, until cooked through. Meanwhile, in a separate saucepan, heat 1 tablespoon olive oil, add 4 sliced red onions, and cook for 2–3 minutes, then stir in 2 teaspoons balsamic vinegar and 1 teaspoon sugar and cook for 5–6 minutes. Meanwhile, cook 2 cups prepared mashed potatoes in a microwave oven according to the package directions, then stir in 2 tablespoons whole-grain mustard. Serve the sausages and onions with the mashed potatoes.

 Sausage and Onion Kebabs with Lemon Mashed Potatoes Cook 5 russet or Yukon gold potatoes, peeled and cut into chunks, in a saucepan of boiling water for 12–15 minutes, until tender. Meanwhile, thread 8 chopped gluten-free sausages, 2 onions, cut into wedges, 2 seeded and chopped red bell peppers, and 1 seeded and chopped yellow bell pepper onto 8 skewers, presoaked in water to prevent them from burning. Brush with 2 tablespoons olive oil and sprinkle with 2 tablespoons chopped rosemary. Place under a preheated hot broiler and cook for 10–12 minutes, turning regularly. Drain the potatoes and mash with 4 tablespoons butter, the grated zest of 1 lemon, and 1 tablespoon crème fraîche or heavy cream. Serve the kebabs with the lemon mashed potatoes and a few sprigs of watercress.

10 Quick Pancetta and Broccoli Pizza

Serves 4

12 slices pancetta

4 gluten-free pita breads

3 cups bite-size baby
broccoli pieces

1¾ cups grated mozzarella cheese

- Place the pancetta under a hot broiler and cook for 4–5 minutes, until crisp.

- Meanwhile, toast the pita breads for 1–2 minutes on each side. Cook the baby broccoli in a saucepan of boiling water for 2 minutes, then drain.

- Place 2 slices of the pancetta on each pita bread and divide the broccoli between them. Sprinkle with the mozzarella and place under the hot broiler for 2–3 minutes, until golden and bubbling.

2 **Fusilli with Purple Baby Broccoli and Pancetta** Cook 8 oz pancetta, cut into strips, in a skillet for 8–10 minutes, then add 4 sliced garlic cloves and cook for another 1 minute. Pour in ¼ cup white wine and simmer for 4–5 minutes. Meanwhile, cook 12 oz gluten-free fusilli in a saucepan of boiling water for 9–12 minutes, or according to the package directions, adding 3½ cups trimmed and chopped purple baby broccoli 2 minutes before the end of the cooking time. Drain the pasta and broccoli, then toss with the pancetta and ½ cup grated Parmesan to serve.

3 **Purple Baby Broccoli, Chile, and Pancetta Pizza** Cook 3½ cups trimmed and halved purple baby broccoli in boiling water for 2–3 minutes. Drain. Spread 2 large gluten-free pizza crusts with ¾ cup prepared pizza sauce. Add the broccoli and sprinkle with 8 oz diced pancetta and 1 teaspoon dried red pepper flakes. Top with ½ red onion, sliced, and 8 oz sliced mozzarella. Bake in a preheated oven, at 425°F, for 22–25 minutes, until golden and bubbling.

20 Liver with Sage Lentils

Serves 4

1 tablespoon olive oil
1 carrot, peeled and diced
1 celery stick, diced
½ small red onion, finely diced
4 sage leaves, coarsely torn
1 garlic clove, sliced
2 cups cooked green lentils
½ cup red wine
4 cups baby spinach leaves
2–3 tablespoons crème fraîche
   or heavy cream
4 unsmoked bacon slices
1 lb liver
salt and black pepper

- Heat the oil in a skillet over medium heat, add the carrot, celery, and onion, and cook for 2–3 minutes, then stir in the sage, garlic, and lentils. Pour in the wine, add the spinach and crème fraîche, and cook for 8–10 minutes.

- Meanwhile, cook the bacon under a preheated medium broiler for 7 minutes or until crisp, then chop coarsely.

- Season the liver with salt and black pepper. Place under a hot broiler or in a hot ridged grill pan and cook for 1–2 minutes on each side.

- Serve the liver on a bed of lentils, sprinkled with the chopped bacon.

 Liver with Onions and Sage Mashed Potatoes Heat 1 tablespoon olive oil in a skillet, add 3 sliced onions, and cook for 6–7 minutes. Add a dash of balsamic vinegar and ½ teaspoon sugar and cook for another 2–3 minutes. In another skillet, cook 1 lb sliced liver in 2 tablespoons butter for 1–2 minutes on each side. Meanwhile, heat 2½ cups prepared mashed potatoes in a microwave oven according to the package directions and stir in 1 tablespoon chopped sage. Divide the potatoes among 4 plates, top with the liver and onions, and serve immediately.

 Cheese and Sage Chicken Livers with Lentil Salad Heat 1 tablespoon olive oil in a saucepan, add 1 diced carrot, 1 diced celery stick, 1 small diced red onion, and 2 sliced garlic cloves, and cook for 2–3 minutes. Add 2 cups cooked lentils and heat through for 2–3 minutes, then remove from the heat. Whisk together 3 tablespoons olive oil, 1 tablespoon red wine vinegar, ½ teaspoon Dijon mustard, and ½ teaspoon honey. In a shallow bowl, mix together ¾ cup cornmeal, 1 cup grated Parmesan, ½ tablespoon chopped sage, and ½ teaspoon pepper. Beat 2 eggs and put into another shallow bowl. Melt 2 tablespoons butter with 1 tablespoon olive oil in a skillet. Dip 1 lb chicken livers first into the egg and then the cornmeal mixture, then add to the pan and cook for 2–3 minutes on each side. Drain on paper towels. Toss the lentils with 6 cups mixed salad greens and the dressing, and top with the liver.

30 Chicken en Papillote with Mashed Potatoes and Celeriac

Serves 4

5 russet or Yukon gold potatoes, peeled and cut into chunks
½ head of celeriac, peeled and cut into chunks
4 (5 oz) chicken breasts
8 tarragon sprigs
½ cup white wine
2 cups trimmed green beans
4 tablespoons butter
salt and black pepper

- Cook the potatoes and celeriac together in a saucepan of boiling water for 10–12 minutes, until tender.

- Meanwhile, place each chicken breast on a large piece of parchment paper. Place 2 tarragon sprigs on each, then sprinkle with 2 tablespoons white wine and black pepper. Fold the paper to securely enclose the chicken and liquid and place the packages on a baking sheet or in a roasting pan.

- Bake in a preheated oven, at 400 °F, for 15–18 minutes.

- Meanwhile, steam the green beans for 3–4 minutes.

- Drain the potatoes and celeriac and mash together with the butter. Season with salt and black pepper.

- Serve the chicken on a bed of mashed poatoes topped with the green beans. Pour over any cooking juices.

---

10 Grilled Chicken with Mashed Potatoes
Flatten 4 (5 oz) chicken breasts with a rolling pin. Mix together ¼ cup lemon juice, 2 tablespoons honey, and 1 tablespoon chopped tarragon and toss the chicken in the mixture. Cook in a hot ridged grill pan for 4 minutes on each side, until cooked through. Meanwhile, boil 2 cups green beans for 3–4 minutes and heat 2½ cups prepared mashed potatoes in a microwave oven according to the package directions. Stir 2 tablespoons butter through the potatoes and serve with the chicken and beans.

20 Mashed Potato-Topped Chicken Pies Heat 1 tablespoon olive oil in a saucepan over medium heat, add 4 (5 oz) chopped skinless, boneless chicken breasts and 1 sliced onion, and cook for 4–5 minutes. Add ⅔ cup chicken stock and cook for another 12–14 minutes. Meanwhile, heat 3 cups prepared mashed potatoes in the microwave oven according to the package directions. Stir 1 (11 oz) can corn kernels, drained, into the chicken mixture with 2 tablespoons crème fraîche or heavy cream,

½ tablespoon chopped tarragon, and 1 tablespoon chopped parsley. Season with salt and black pepper and spoon into 4 individual pie dishes. Top with the mashed potatoes and serve.

Stir-Fried Mixed Vegetables with Cashew Nuts

Serves 4

2 tablespoons peanut oil

½ cup cashew nuts

¾ inch piece of fresh ginger root, peeled and finely chopped

3½ cups shredded napa cabbage or green cabbage

½ cup cauliflower florets

1 cup broccoli florets

1 red bell pepper, seeded and sliced

6 baby corn, halved lengthwise

4 garlic cloves, chopped

1 tablespoon tamari soy sauce

- Heat the oil in a wok over high heat, add the cashew nuts and ginger, and stir-fry for 1 minute.

- Mix together the remaining ingredients in a bowl, then throw into the wok and cook over high heat for 4–5 minutes, stirring and turning continuously. Serve immediately.

 Cashew Nut Pâté with Vegetable Crudites Heat ½ tablespoon olive oil in a skillet over high heat, add 2 cups diced cremini mushrooms, and cook for 3–4 minutes. Add 1½ cups cashew nuts and cook for another 3–4 minutes. Transfer to a food processor with 2 sliced scallions, 1 tablespoon tahini paste, 2 tablespoons olive oil, 1 tablespoon plain yogurt, and salt and black pepper. Blend until nearly smooth. Adjust the seasoning, if necessary, and serve with vegetable crudites.

 Vegetable and Cashew Curry Toast ⅔ cup cashew nuts in a dry skillet over medium heat for 2–3 minutes, then transfer to a bowl and set aside. Heat 1 tablespoon sunflower oil in the skillet, add 1 chopped onion, and cook for 2–3 minutes. Add 1 seeded and chopped red bell pepper, 2 cups snow peas, 1 cup broccoli florets, and 8 baby corn and cook, stirring, for 2–3 minutes. Stir in 1 tablespoon Thai curry paste and 1¾ cups coconut milk and simmer for 12–15 minutes, until the vegetables are tender. Stir in half of the toasted cashew nuts. Serve on warm plates, sprinkled with the remaining nuts.

QuickCook
Sweet Things and Baking

Recipes listed by cooking time

30

20

10

3⊙ Sweet Orange Pancakes

Serves 4

1⅔ cups gluten-free flour blend
2 eggs
1¼ cups milk
½ tablespoon sunflower oil,
 for oiling
2 oranges
2–3 tablespoons sugar, to serve

- Sift the flour into a bowl and make a well in the center.

- Add the eggs and whisk, using a handheld electric mixer, while gradually adding the milk and bringing the flour into the batter. Let stand for 10 minutes.

- Heat a small skillet over medium heat. Lightly oil the pan by wiping it with an oiled sheet of paper towel.

- Pour a generous tablespoon of the batter into the skillet and roll it around to completely coat the bottom of the pan. Cook for 3–4 minutes then turn over and cook the other side for 2–3 minutes.

- Place on a piece of wax paper and keep warm. Repeat with the remaining batter to make 8 pancakes.

- Grate the orange zest, then segment the oranges, catching the juice. Pour the juice into a saucepan, add the segments and zest, and warm through. Pour the orange sauce over the pancakes to serve, with a sprinkling of sugar.

 Sweet Orange Drop Scones Whisk 1⅔ cups gluten-free flour blend, 1½ teaspoons gluten-free baking powder, 2 eggs, and 2 teaspoons sugar with 1¼ cups milk. Heat a little sunflower oil in a skillet, add spoonfuls of the batter to the pan, and cook for 1–2 minutes. When air bubbles start to show on the surface, flip the scones over and cook for another 1–2 minutes on the other side. Stir the grated zest of 2 oranges through 1 cup plain yogurt and serve with the scones.

Sweet Orange Scones

Sift together 2 cups gluten-free flour blend and 1 tablespoon gluten-free baking powder. Rub in 4 tablespoons butter until the mixture resembles fine bread crumbs, then stir in ¼ cup superfine or granulated sugar and the grated zest of 1 orange. Lightly beat together 1 egg and ½ cup milk and stir into the flour mixture to make a soft dough. Turn out onto a lightly floured work surface and lightly press until about ¾ inch

thick. Using a 1½ inch cutter, cut into 8–10 circles and place on a baking sheet. Bake in a preheated oven, at 400°F, for 15–16 minutes, until risen and lightly browned. Serve warm spread with butter or a dollop of cream.

10 Petit Desserts au Chocolat

Serves 4

6 oz semisweet chocolate,
coarsely chopped
1 tablespoon brandy
1 cup heavy cream
¼ cup crème fraîche
unsweetened cocoa powder,
for dusting

- Put the chocolate into a heatproof bowl set over a saucepan of gently simmering water and stir until melted.

- Warm the brandy and cream in a small saucepan over medium heat until hot but not boiling. Stir into the chocolate until completely blended.

- Spoon the chocolate mixture into 4 cups or ramekins and chill until firm.

- Serve topped with a dollop of crème fraîche and dusted with cocoa powder.

20 Molten chocolate Desserts

In a heatproof bowl set over a saucepan of gently simmering water, melt together 6 oz semisweet chocolate and 1¼ sticks butter, stirring occasionally until smooth. In another bowl, whisk together 2 eggs and 2 egg yolks with 2 tablespoons granulated sugar. Whisk in the chocolate mixture, then sift in 2 teaspoons gluten-free flour blend and fold it in. Divide the mixture among 4 dessert molds or ramekin dishes and bake in a preheated oven, at 400°F, for 9–10 minutes, until cooked on the outside but still soft inside. Serve warm.

30 Chocolate Muffins

In a large bowl, mix together 1⅔ cups gluten-free flour blend, 1½ teaspoons gluten-free baking powder, ¼ cup unsweetened cocoa powder, and 1 cup granulated sugar. Rub in 1 stick unsalted butter until the mixture resembles fine bread crumbs. Whisk together 2 eggs and ½ cup milk, then stir into the flour mixture. Line a 12-section muffin pan with paper liners, spoon in the batter, and bake in a preheated oven, at 400°F, for 20 minutes, until risen.

30 Coconut and Raspberry Muffins

Serves 4

1¾ cups gluten-free flour blend

2¾ teaspoons gluten-free baking powder

½ teaspoon baking soda

⅓ cup superfine or granulated sugar

½ cup dry shredded coconut

4 tablespoons unsalted butter, melted

2 eggs

⅔ cup milk

1 cup raspberries

- Line a 12-section muffin pan with paper muffin liners.
- In a large bowl, sift together the flour, baking powder, and baking soda, then mix in the sugar and coconut. Make a well in the center.
- Whisk together the melted butter, eggs, and milk.
- Add the wet ingredients to the dry and mix together gently, adding the raspberries when nearly combined; do not overmix.
- Spoon into the paper liners. Bake in a preheated oven, at 400°F, for 15 minutes, until golden and slightly risen.
- Cool on a wire rack.

 Coconut and Raspberry Yogurt Puddings Toast ¼ cup dry shredded coconut under a preheated medium broiler for 3–4 minutes, until lightly golden. Stir into 2 cups plain yogurt with 1 cup raspberries. Divide among 4 small bowls or glasses and serve sprinkled with a few raspberries on top and a drizzle of honey.

 Coconut Scones with Raspberries Sift 2 cups gluten-free flour blend into a bowl with 1 tablespoon gluten-free baking powder. Stir in 1 tablespoon dry shredded coconut. Rub in 4 tablespoons unsalted butter until the mixture resembles fine bread crumbs. Stir in ¼ cup superfine or granulated sugar. Whisk together 1 egg and ⅔ cup milk and pour this into the flour mixture. Bring the dough together. Using an ice cream scoop, scoop 8 mounds of the dough onto a baking sheet. Bake in a preheated oven, at 425°F, for 12–15 minutes, until risen and golden. Serve warm with crème fraîche or butter and some fresh raspberries.

 # Caramelized Pears with Salted Caramel Sauce

Serves 4

1 stick unsalted butter
½ cup firmly packed light
   brown sugar
¼ cup granulated sugar
3 tablespoons light corn syrup
½ cup heavy cream
1 teaspoon salt flakes
4 pears, peeled, halved, and cored

- To make the salted caramel sauce, put 6 tablespoons of the butter, a firmly packed ⅓ cup of the light brown sugar, the granulated sugar, and corn syrup in a small, heavy saucepan. Put over low heat to melt, stirring until the sugar has dissolved, then simmer for 3 minutes, stirring occasionally.

- Stir in the cream and half the salt. Carefully taste the caramel sauce, then add more salt, if desired. Pour into a small bowl to cool a little.

- Meanwhile, melt the remaining butter and sugar in a skillet, add the pears, and cook for 4–5 minutes, until golden.

- Serve with the salted caramel sauce.

2 Apple and Pear Fritters with Salted Caramel Sauce

Put 1¼ cups gluten-free flour blend in a bowl and whisk in 2 eggs, 2 egg yolks and 1 cup milk. Whisk 2 egg whites until they just start to hold their shape, then fold into the batter. Peel, halve, and core 2 pears and 2 sweet, crisp apples, then cut into wedges. Put 1 tablespoon vegetable oil in a heavy saucepan over medium heat and heat until a small piece of bread dropped into the oil sizzles and turns golden within 20 seconds. In 3–4 batches, dip the fruit into the batter, then carefully cook in the oil for 3–4 minutes, until golden and crisp. Remove, using a slotted spoon, drain on paper towels, and toss with 1 teaspoon ground cinnamon and ⅔ cup granulated sugar. Serve with some Salted Caramel Sauce, made as above.

3 Pear Muffins with Salted Caramel

Sift together 1¾ cups gluten-free flour blend, 2¾ teaspoons gluten-free baking powder, and ½ teaspoon baking soda. Stir in ⅓ cup sugar and make a well in the center. Whisk together 4 tablespoons butter, melted, 2 eggs, and ⅔ cup milk. Pour the wet ingredients into the dry and mix gently, then stir in 2 peeled, cored, and diced pears. Line a 12-section muffin pan with paper liners and spoon the batter into the liners. Bake in a preheated oven, at 400°F, for 15 minutes, until risen and golden. Meanwhile, make the Salted Caramel Sauce as above. Serve the muffins warm with the sauce.

20 Rhubarb Whip

Serves 4

9 rhubarb stalks, chopped
 into bite-size pieces
2 tablespoons granulated sugar
¼ cup white wine
1¼ cups heavy cream
finely grated zest of 1 lemon
1 egg white
chopped pistachios nuts, to serve

- Put the rhubarb and sugar into a saucepan over low heat, pour in the wine, and simmer over low heat until cooked. Pour into a bowl and let cool.

- Whisk the cream until thick and stir into the rhubarb with the grated lemon zest.

- Whisk the egg white until stiff, then gently fold into the rhubarb mixture.

- Divide among 4 bowls and top with the chopped pistachios. Chill until required.

---

10 Quick Rhubarb Whip

Blend 2 cups canned rhubarb pie filling in a food processor to make a puree. Whisk 1¼ cups heavy cream with the grated zest of 1 lemon, then fold in the rhubarb puree. Taste for sweetness, adding a little honey to taste. Divide among 4 glasses and serve.

30 Roasted Rhubarb

Cut 10 rhubarb stalks into finger-size pieces. Put into a shallow ovenproof dish and toss with ⅓ cup granulated sugar, making sure the rhubarb is in a single layer. Cover with aluminum foil and roast in a preheated oven, at 400°F, for 15 minutes. Remove the foil and continue to cook for another 5–6 minutes, until the rhubarb is tender and the juices are syrupy. Serve with vanilla ice cream.

30 Tropical Salsa with Ice Cream

Serves 4

1 passion fruit
1 ripe mango, pitted, peeled, and finely diced
½ cup finely diced pineapple
1 piece of preserved ginger, finely diced
1 teaspoon preserved ginger syrup
1 teaspoon finely shredded mint
½ teaspoon finely shredded cilantro leaves
ice cream of your choice, to serve

- Halve the passion fruit and scoop the pulp into a strainer placed over a bowl and press the seeds to get all the juice out. Discard the seeds.

- Add the finely diced fruit and ginger to the bowl, then stir in the ginger syrup.

- Finally, stir in the shredded herbs. Let stand at room temperature for 20 minutes to let the flavors mingle.

- When ready to serve, spoon the salsa over your favorite ice cream for an instant tropical dessert.

---

1 Tropical Fruits and Meringue

Put 2 individual broken meringue nests into a large bowl and add ½ cup diced pineapple, 1 peeled, pitted, and diced mango and 1¼ cups plain yogurt. Stir in 1 diced piece of preserved ginger and ½ tablespoon chopped mint. Mix gently so you do not break up the meringue pieces too much. Divide among 4 small glasses or bowls to serve.

2 Tropical Winter Fruit Salad

Put 10 peeled and pitted litchis into a large bowl with 1 small pineapple, peeled and cut into chunks, 1 peeled and pitted mango, cut into chunks, the seeds of 1 pomegranate, and 6 diced medjool dates. Scrape the pulp from 3 passion fruit and strain to remove the seeds. Gently stir the passion fruit juice through the salad and check to

see if any sweetness is required; if so, add a little honey. Let sit at room temperature for a few minutes, then serve with dollops of crème fraîche, Greek yogurt, or whipped cream sprinkled with ground nutmeg.

30 Baked Apples with Spiced Fruit

Serves 4

4 cooking apples, such as Granny
  Smith or Pippin, cored and
  scored around the middle
½ cup dried cranberries
4 pieces of preserved ginger,
  diced
finely grated zest of 2 oranges
½ teaspoon allspice
¼ cup honey
crème fraîche, to serve

- Put the apples into an ovenproof dish. Mix together the cranberries, ginger, orange zest, allspice, and honey and spoon the mixture into the cavity of each apple.

- Pour 2 tablespoons water into the dish. Bake in a preheated oven, at 375°F, for 22–25 minutes, until the apples are puffy and cooked through. Serve with crème fraîche.

---

1 Spiced Apples

Melt 2 tablespoons butter in a skillet over medium heat, add 4 peeled, cored, and sliced crisp apples and ½ tablespoon allspice, and cook for 5–6 minutes. Stir in 2 tablespoons honey and serve with crème fraîche.

2 Spiced Apple Scones

Sift 2 cups gluten-free flour blend into a bowl with 1 tablespoon gluten-free baking powder and ½ teaspoon ground cinnamon. Rub in 4 tablespoons unsalted butter until the mixture resembles fine bread crumbs. Stir in ¼ cup granulated sugar. Whisk together 1 egg and ⅔ cup milk and pour into the flour mixture. Bring the dough together. Using an ice cream scoop, scoop 8 mounds of dough onto a baking sheet. Bake in a preheated oven, at 425°F, for 12–15 minutes, until risen and golden. Meanwhile, melt 2 tablespoons butter in a saucepan, add 2 cored and sliced sweet, crisp apples, and cook for 3–4 minutes. Remove from the heat and sprinkle with 2 teaspoons granulated sugar and ¼ teaspoon ground cinnamon. Serve the scones split in half and topped with a little apple and a dollop of crème fraîche.

 # Blueberry and Date Mousse

Serves 4

½ cups dates
½ cup pitted prunes
grated zest of 1 orange
2 tablespoons crème fraîche
3–4 tablespoons plain yogurt
⅔ cup blueberries
grated semisweet chocolate,
  to serve

- Put the dates and prunes into a food processor with the orange zest and process until broken down.

- Add the crème fraîche, yogurt, and blueberries and process again until you have a mousselike texture.

- Spoon into 4 glasses and sprinkle with a little grated chocolate to serve.

 ### Blueberry and Date Oat Bars

In a heavy saucepan, melt together ½ cup coconut oil, ¼ cup molasses, 1 tablespoon packed dark brown sugar, and 3 tablespoons agave syrup until the sugar has dissolved. Stir in 2¾ cups rolled oats, ½ cup dried blueberries, and ⅓ cup chopped dates. Spoon into a lightly greased 7 inch cake pan and bake in a preheated oven, at 350°F, for 15–16 minutes. Let cool for 2 minutes, then cut into squares and let cool completely in the pan.

 ### Blueberry and Date Muffins

Sift together 1¾ cups gluten-free flour blend with 1 tablespoon gluten-free baking powder and ½ teaspoon baking soda. Stir in ⅓ cup sugar and make a well in the center. Whisk together 4 tablespoons unsalted butter, melted, 2 eggs, and ⅔ cup milk. Add the wet ingredients to the dry and mix together gently, adding 1 cup blueberries when nearly mixed; do not overmix. Line a 12-section muffin pan with paper liners, spoon in the batter, and bake in a preheated oven, at 400°F, for 15 minutes, until risen and golden. Remove from the pan and cool on a wire rack or serve warm.

30 Amaretti-Stuffed Peaches

Serves 4

4 ripe peaches, halved and pitted
8 amaretti cookies, crushed
¼ cup mascarpone cheese
grated zest and juice of 1 orange

- Put the peaches into a shallow ovenproof dish, cut side up.

- Mix together the crushed cookies, mascarpone, and orange zest and divide the mixture into the halved peaches.

- Sprinkle with the orange juice and bake in a preheated oven, at 400°F, for 15–20 minutes, until tender.

 Quick Peach Amaretti Pudding

Mix together 1 cup Greek yogurt with 1 cup mascarpone cheese. Stir in the grated zest of 1 orange and 6 crushed amaretti cookies. Pit and slice 4 peaches, divide among 4 plates, and serve each one with a generous dollop of the amaretti cream.

 Amaretti and Peach Trifle

Put 1 (7 oz) package amaretti cookies into a glass bowl. Top with 6 pitted and chopped peaches and drizzle with ½ cup Amaretto liqueur. Pour 1¾ cups prepared custard or vanilla pudding and pie filling over the top to cover. Whisk 1¼ cups heavy cream to soft peaks and spoon it over the trifle. Sprinkle with ½ cup toasted slivered almonds. Chill for 10 minutes before serving.

30 Florentines

Serves 4

4 tablespoons unsalted butter
½ cup granulated sugar
¼ cup thick heavy cream
1¾ cups slivered almonds
2 tablespoons chopped
   candied peel
1 egg white
4 semisweet chocolate, melted

- Line 2 baking sheets with parchment paper.

- Put the butter and sugar into a small saucepan with ¼ cup water. Bring to a boil, then cook ver high heat for 5 minutes, until the mixture starts to turn pale. Remove from the heat and let cook for 2 minutes.

- Stir in the cream, almonds, and candied peel.

- Whisk the egg white to soft peaks, then gently fold into the almond mixture.

- Spoon the dough onto the prepared baking sheets to make 12 Florentines, leaving space between each one.

- Bake in a preheated oven, at 350°F, for 15–18 minutes, until golden. Carefully slide onto a wire rack and let cool.

- Spread the bottom of each Florentine with melted chocolate and let set.

 Almond and Candied Peel

Muesli Mix together 2¼ cups rolled oats, 1 cup mixed dried fruits (including chopped candied peel), and 1 cup slivered almonds. Serve with milk, plain yogurt, and fresh fruit.

 Orange and Almond Muffins

Mix together 1¾ cups gluten-free flour blend, 1 tablespoon gluten-free baking powder, ½ teaspoon baking soda, ⅓ cup granulated sugar, ½ cup diced candied peel, the grated zest of 1 orange, and ½ cup slivered almonds. Whisk together 4 tablespoons butter, melted, 2 eggs, and ⅔ cup milk and pour into the dry ingredients. Line a 12-section muffin pan with paper liners, spoon in the batter, and bake in a preheated oven, at 400°F, for 15 minutes, until golden.

GLU-SWEE-LAW

 # Spicy Grilled Pineapple

Serves 4

8 slices of fresh pineapple,
  peeled and cored
1 tablespoon honey
pinch of dried red pepper flakes
pinch of ground cinnamon
crème fraîche or plain yogurt,
  to serve

- Heat a skillet or ridged grill pan until hot. Add the pineapple slices and cook until they start to caramelize. Turn them over just once.

- Add the honey, red pepper flakes, and cinnamon and cook until the mixture starts to bubble; this will not take long.

- Serve the pineapple slices drizzled with the spicy honey and a dollop of crème fraîche or plain yogurt.

 ### Spicy Pineapple Smoothie

Coarsely chop 1 small, peeled pineapple and 1 banana and place in a blender with 2 teaspoons honey, a pinch of dried red pepper flakes, and a pinch of cinnamon. Pour in 1¾ cups milk and 2–3 tablespoons plain yogurt and blend until smooth, adding more milk, if needed, to make a thick creamy smoothie.

Pineapple Fritters

Make the batter by putting 1 cup gluten-free flour blend into a bowl with ¼ cup granulated sugar and a pinch of salt. Add 1 egg, 1 egg yolk, and ⅔ cup milk and whisk to make a smooth batter. In another clean bowl, whisk 1 egg white until it forms stiff peaks and gently fold into the batter. Let the batter stand for 10 minutes. Heat 2 cups sunflower oil in a saucepan until a small cube of bread sizzles and browns when dropped into the oil. Peel, core, and slice 1 pineapple into slices. Dip the pineapple slices into the batter and cook in the oil in batches for 3–4 minutes, until golden on both sides. Remove from the pan and drain on paper towels. Sprinkle with confectioners' sugar. Serve with a dollop of plain yogurt or crème fraîche, with a sprinkling of grated nutmeg or ground cinnamon.

30 Sticky Rice and Mango

Serves 4

1¼ cups long-grain rice
1 cup coconut milk
¼ cup granulated sugar
4–5 cardamom pods, bruised
2 mangoes, pitted, peeled,
  and sliced

- Wash the rice in a few changes of water, then let soak for 10 minutes.

- Drain the rice and place in a saucepan with 1¼ cups water. Bring to a boil and let boil for 1 minute. Reduce the heat, cover, and let simmer for 8–9 minutes, until all the water has been absorbed.

- Meanwhile, mix together the coconut milk and sugar. Add the bruised cardamom pods.

- Pour the coconut mixture into the rice and slowly bring to a boil, then simmer for 10 minutes, stirring occasionally; do not let it stick. Turn off the heat and let stand for 5 minutes.

- Serve the sticky rice with slices of fresh mango.

 Quick Cardamom Rice Pudding with Mango In a saucepan, heat the crushed seeds of 4–5 cardamom pods with 2–3 tablespoons heavy cream to steep the cream with the cardamom flavor. Stir in 1 (15 oz) can of rice pudding and heat according to the directions on the label. Meanwhile, heat 1 tablespoon honey in a skillet, add 2 pitted, peeled, and sliced mangoes, and cook for 3–4 minutes, until starting to caramelize. Serve the mango with the cardamom rice pudding.

 Mango and Cardamom Muffins Sift together 1¾ cups gluten-free flour blend with 1 tablespoon gluten-free baking powder and ½ teaspoon baking soda. Stir in ⅓ cup superfine or granulated sugar and the crushed seeds of 4–5 cardamom pods. Whisk together 4 tablespoons unsalted butter, melted, 2 eggs, and ⅔ cup milk. Pour the wet ingredients into the dry and mix gently, adding 1 pitted, peeled, and diced mango when nearly mixed; do not overmix. Bake in a preheated oven, at 400°F, for 12–15 minutes, until risen and golden.

GLU-SWEE-QEO

10 Chile Hot Chocolate

Serves 4

6 oz semisweet chocolate,
broken into pieces
1 large pinch of chili powder
2 tablespoons superfine or
granulated sugar
2 large pinches of ground
cinnamon
2 vanilla beans, split lengthwise
2½ cups milk
1 cup heavy cream, whipped
grated semisweet chocolate,
to serve

- Put the chocolate, chili powder, sugar, cinnamon, vanilla beans, and milk into a saucepan and heat gently until the chocolate has melted.

- Bring to a boil and whisk until the chocolate is smooth and frothy.

- Remove the vanilla beans.

- Pour the chocolate into 4 warm mugs and top with the whipped cream and grated chocolate.

 Chile Chocolate Mousse

Put 5 oz semisweet chocolate and ¼ seeded and finely diced red chile into a food processor and process until chopped. Add 2 eggs and blend until nearly smooth. While the machine is running, pour in ⅔ cup hot coffee and continue to blend until the mousse is completely smooth. Taste for sweetness and, if needed, add 1 teaspoon honey and blend again. Pour into 4 small glasses or bowls and place in the freezer for 15 minutes to set.

 Chile Chocolate Cupcakes

Beat together 2 sticks butter, softened, 1¼ cups granulated sugar, and ¼ seeded and finely diced red chile until light and fluffy. Add 4 beaten eggs, one at a time, adding a little of 2 cups gluten-free flour blend after each egg. Stir in the remaining flour, 2 teaspoons gluten-free baking powder, and 3 tablespoons unsweetened cocoa powder, then spoon the batter into 12 paper liners in a 12-section cupcake pan. Bake in a preheated oven, at 375°F, for 20 minutes. Remove from the pan, place on a wire rack, and sprinkle with 4 oz grated semisweet chocolate and 1 oz grated white chocolate.

 # Fruit-Stuffed Pancakes

Serves 4

¾ cup rice flour

1 teaspoon gluten-free
  baking powder

½ teaspoon ground cinnamon

1 egg

finely grated zest of 1 lemon

¾ cup soy milk

2–3 teaspoons sunflower oil

1 peach, pitted and chopped

⅔ cup blueberries

½ cup raspberries

¼ cantaloupe, seeded
  and chopped

5–6 mint leaves, shredded

¼ cup honey

plain yogurt, to serve

- Put the flour, baking powder, cinnamon, egg, lemon zest, and milk into a food processor, add 2–3 tablespoons water, and blend together.

- Heat half the oil in a skillet over medium heat, pour in one-quarter of the batter, and cook for 2–3 minutes, then flip the pancake over and cook for another 1–2 minutes. Remove from the pan and keep warm. Repeat with the remaining batter, adding more oil to the pan, if needed.

- Gently mix together the fruit. Spoon one-quarter of the fruit mixture into the middle of each pancake and sprinkle over some shredded mint. Fold the pancakes in half and place on a baking sheet. Drizzle with the honey and cook under a preheated hot broiler for 2–3 minutes. Serve with a dollop of yogurt.

Fruit Smoothie

In a blender, blend together 1 chopped banana, 2 pitted and chopped peaches, ½ cantaloupe, seeded and chopped, ¾ cup raspberries, 1 cup plain yogurt, 2½ cups soy milk, and 2–3 tablespoons honey. If desired, add a few ice cubes, and blend again.

Baked Mint Fruit Compote

Pit 3 peaches, 4 apricots, and 4 plums and cut into wedges. Put into an ovenproof dish with 1⅓ cups blueberries and 1¾ cups raspberries. Blend ¼ cup superfine or granulated sugar with 10–12 mint leaves, then toss the green sugar mixture into the fruit. Bake in a preheated oven, at 375°F, for 22–25 minutes. Serve with plain yogurt.

30 Blackberry and Apple Crisps

Serves 4

4 sweet, crisp apples, peeled, cored, and thinly sliced

1 cup blackberries

2 teaspoons superfine or granulated sugar

1 cup rolled oats

4 tablespoons unsalted butter, diced

⅓ cup firmly packed dark brown sugar

¼ cup slivered almonds

- Divide the apple slices and blackberries among 4 small ovenproof dishes or ramekins and sprinkle with the superfine or granulated sugar.

- In a food processor, blend the oats, butter, brown sugar, and almonds. Spoon the oat mixture over the fruit and bake in a preheated oven, at 375°F, for 22–25 minutes, until golden.

 Blackberry and Apple Whip

Whip 1¼ cups heavy cream until soft peaks form. Gently fold in ⅔ cup applesauce and 1 cup lightly crushed blackberries. Divide among 4 glasses and chill until ready to serve.

 Blackberry and Apple Muffins

Sift together 1¾ cups gluten-free flour blend, 1 tablespoon gluten-free baking powder, and ½ teaspoon baking soda. Stir in ⅓ cup granulated sugar and make a well in the center. Whisk together 4 tablespoons unsalted butter, melted, 2 eggs, and ⅔ cup milk. Add the wet ingredients to the dry and mix together gently, adding ⅔ cup blackberries and 1 peeled, cored, and diced sweet, crisp apple when nearly combined; do not overmix. Divide among 12 paper muffin liners in a muffin pan and bake in a preheated oven, at 400°F, for 15 minutes, until risen and golden. Cool on a wire rack or eat warm.

30 Date and Amaretti Tiramisu

Serves 4

6 dates, pitted and coarsely
 chopped
½ cup strong coffee
¼ cup Amaretto liqueur
2 eggs, separated
⅓ cup superfine sugar
⅔ cup mascarpone cheese
½ cup ricotta cheese
⅔ cup heavy cream,
 whipped to soft peaks
24 amaretti cookies,
 lightly crushed
3 tablespoons unsweetened
 cocoa powder

- Put the dates in a saucepan with the coffee and bring to a boil, then remove from the heat, stir in the Amaretto liqueur, and let cool for 15 minutes.

- Whisk the egg whites and 2 tablespoons of the superfine sugar to stiff peaks.

- In a separate bowl, whisk the remaining sugar with the mascarpone, ricotta, and egg yolks, then fold in the whipped cream. Finally, fold in the egg whites.

- Toss the amaretti cookies with the dates, then spoon one-half of this mixture into 4 glasses. Sift over one-third of the cocoa powder.

- Top with one-half of the cream mixture, then repeat the layers with the remaining ingredients.

- Finish off with a sifting of cocoa powder. Chill until ready to serve.

 ### Date and Coffee Desserts

In a small saucepan, bring ½ cup strong coffee, 2 teaspoons granulated sugar, 12 crushed cardamom pods, and 1 cinnamon stick to a boil. Add 2½ cups pitted dates, then remove from the heat and let stand for 8 minutes. Spoon the dates into 4 glasses, top with 1½ cups Greek yogurt, and sift over 1 tablespoon unsweetened cocoa powder to serve.

 ### Date and Coffee Cakes

Lightly grease a 12-section muffin pan. Put 2 cups pitted and chopped dates in a small saucepan with 1 cup weak coffee. Bring to a boil, then remove from the heat and stir in 1 teaspoon baking soda. Add 5 tablespoons unsalted butter and stir until it has melted. Sift 1⅓ cups gluten-free flour blend into a bowl, then stir in ½ cup firmly packed dark brown sugar. Make a well in the center, pour in the date mixture and 2 beaten eggs, and mix together well. Spoon into the prepared muffin pan and cook in a preheated oven, at 350°F, for 15–18 minutes. Meanwhile, put 1 stick unsalted butter, ⅔ cup firmly packed light brown sugar, 2 tablespoons light corn syrup, and ¾ cup heavy cream into a saucepan over low heat and cook, stirring, for 3–4 minutes. Bring to a boil and then simmer for 2 minutes. To serve, turn the cakes out onto serving plates, pour over the sauce, and top with vanilla ice cream.

 # Strawberries and Meringue with Ginger

Serves 4

3 cups hulled and chopped strawberries

1 teaspoon ginger syrup

1¾ cups heavy cream

3 prepared meringue nests, lightly crushed

2 pieces of preserved ginger, diced

1 tablespoon shredded mint

- Toss the strawberries in a bowl with the ginger syrup.

- Whip the cream to soft peaks, then stir in the strawberries, crushed meringue, ginger, and half the shredded mint.

- Divide among 4 glasses and sprinkle with the remaining shredded mint to serve.

 ### Strawberry Cheesecakes

Melt 2 tablespoons unsalted butter in a small saucepan, then stir in 14 crushed amaretti cookies. Spoon the cookie mixture into 4 ramekins and press into the bottom. Chill for 5 minutes. Mix together 1 cup Greek yogurt, 1 cup cream cheese, 2 teaspoons superfine or granulated sugar, and 2 teaspoons chopped mint. Spoon the yogurt mixture over the cookie crust and level with a knife. Lightly crush 1 cup hulled and diced strawberries and spoon them over the cheesecakes to serve.

 ### Mint-Marinated Strawberries

Put 1⅓ cups hulled and halved strawberries into a bowl with ¼ cup superfine or granulated sugar and 2 tablespoons lemon juice. Lightly mash with a fork, then stir in another 1⅓ cups hulled and halved strawberries. Stir in 2 finely diced pieces of preserved ginger and 2 teaspoons finely chopped mint and let marinate in the refrigerater for 25 minutes. Serve with whipped cream.

30 Chocolate Walnut Brownies

Serves 4

2 sticks unsalted butter

8 oz semisweet chocolate, chopped

1 cup granulated sugar

3 eggs, beaten

1½ cups ground almonds (almond meal)

1 cup chopped walnuts

vanilla ice cream, to serve

- Melt the butter and chocolate together in a small saucepan over low heat. Stir in the sugar.

- Beat the eggs into the pan, then stir in the almonds and walnuts.

- Pour into a 9 inch square cake pan and bake in a preheated oven, at 350°F, for 25 minutes, until the top is set but the middle is still gooey.

- Serve warm with scoops of vanilla ice cream.

 Quick Chocolate Walnut Mousse

Coarsely chop 4 oz semisweet chocolate and put into a bowl. Pour ⅔ cup heavy cream into a small saucepan and bring to a boil. Stir the hot cream into the chocolate to melt it, then pour in another ⅔ cup cold heavy cream and 2 tablespoons Amaretto liqueur. Beat the chocolate mixture with a handheld electric mixer until it forms soft peaks. In another grease-free bowl, whisk 1 extra-large egg white and gradually add ¼ cup superfine sugar, whisking until you have a soft meringue. Fold into the chocolate mixture, then spoon into glasses to serve. Serve sprinkled with 1 tablespoon toasted and chopped walnuts.

 Chocolate Walnut Puddings

Melt together 5 oz chopped semisweet chocolate and 1¼ sticks unsalted butter in a heatproof bowl set over a saucepan of gently simmering water. Remove from the heat, add ⅔ cup warm water and ½ cup superfine or granulated sugar, and stir until smooth. Lightly beat 4 egg yolks and whisk into the chocolate mixture. Fold in 2½ tablespoons rice flour, sifted, ¼ cup toasted and finely chopped walnuts, and 1 teaspoon gluten-free baking powder. Whisk 4 egg whites in a grease-free bowl until stiff, then gently fold into the chocolate mixture. Pour into 4 greased ramekins. Bake in a preheated oven, at 400°F, for 12–15 minutes, until the top is firm and the middle still soft and fudgy. Serve with a dollop of crème fraîche, dusted with unsweetened cocoa powder.

30 Lemon Yogurt Cupcakes

Makes 12

1⅓ cups gluten-free flour blend
½ teaspoon gluten-free
  baking powder
¾ cup granulated sugar
1¼ sticks unsalted butter, melted
2 eggs
¼ cup plain yogurt
grated zest of 2 lemons

For the frosting

1½ sticks unsalted butter,
  softened
3¼ cups confectioners' sugar,
  sifted
grated zest of 1 lemon,
  plus extra for sprinkling

- Line a 12-section muffin pan with paper liners.

- In a bowl, sift together the flour and baking powder, then stir in the sugar.

- Whisk together the melted butter, eggs, yogurt, and lemon zest. Pour into the dry ingredients and mix lightly until combined.

- Divide the batter between the paper liners. Bake in a preheated oven, at 350°F, for 15–18 minutes, until golden. Let cool on a wire rack.

- Beat together the softened butter, confectioners' sugar, and grated lemon zest.

- Pipe or spoon the frosting onto the cupcakes and sprinkle with extra grated lemon zest.

 Lemon Yogurt Dessert

Stir 3 tablespoons lemon curd and the grated zest of 1 lemon into 2 cups Greek yogurt. Divide among 4 glasses, sprinkle with 4 teaspoons dark brown sugar and chill for 5 minutes.

 Lemon Cakes with Greek Yogurt

Spoon 1 teaspoon lemon curd into 4 ramekins. Put 1 cup gluten-free flour blend, ⅔ cup granulated sugar, and 1 stick butter, softened, into a food processor, add 2 tablespoons gluten-free baking powder, 2 eggs, and the grated zest of 1 lemon, and process. Divide the batter among the 4 ramekins. Bake in a preheated oven, at 375°F, for 16–18 minutes. Serve with a dollop of Greek yogurt and grated lemon zest.

20 Banana-Caramel Pie

Serves 4

1 (7 oz) package amaretti cookies,
 lightly crushed

1 stick unsalted butter, melted

1⅔ cups dulce de leche
 (caramel sauce)

3 bananas, sliced

1 cup heavy cream

2 oz semisweet chocolate, grated

- Put the crushed amaretti cookies into a bowl, pour the melted butter over them, and mix well.

- Pour the buttered crumbs into an 8 inch loose-bottom tart pan and press then into the bottom and sides. Chill for 10 minutes.

- Spread the caramel over the cookie crust, then top with the sliced bananas.

- Whip the cream to soft peaks and spread over the bananas.

- Sprinkle the grated chocolate over the top.

 Banana Caramel Desserts

Carefully stir 1⅔ cup of dulce de leche (caramel sauce) into 1⅔ cups Greek yogurt to create a marbled effect. Layer with 3 sliced bananas in 4 glasses and serve sprinkled with 1½ tablespoons grated semisweet chocolate.

 Banana Butterscoth Trifle

Put ⅔ cup light corn syrup, 4 tablespoons unsalted butter, ⅓ cup firmly packed dark brown sugar, and ¼ cup granulated sugar into a small saucepan over low heat and heat for 5–6 minutes, stirring from time to time, until the sugars have dissolved. Cook for 2–3 minutes, then gradually stir in ⅔ cup heavy cream. Let cool for 5–6 minutes. Meanwhile, put 1 (7 oz) package amaretti cookies in a trifle dish and pour over 2–3 tablespoons Amaretto liqueur. Let stand for 5 minutes, then gently stir in 3 chopped bananas. Pour the butterscotch sauce over the cookies and let stand for 5–6 minutes. Spoon 1¼ cups prepared custard on top and chill for 3–4 minutes, then spread with 1 cup whipped cream. Sprinkle with 2 tablespoons grated chocolate to finish.

30 Banana and Honey Oat Bars

Serves 4

oil, for greasing
2 tablespoons packed light
  brown sugar
1½ sticks unsalted butter
1 tablespoon honey
1½ tablespoons light corn syrup
1 large banana, mashed
3 cups rolled oats
1 cup dried banana chips,
  coarsely broken.

- Lightly grease an 8½ inch square cake pan.

- Put the sugar, butter, honey, and corn syrup into a saucepan over medium heat and heat, stirring occasionally, until the butter has melted and the sugar dissolved. Remove from the heat.

- Stir in the mashed banana and oats and mix well. Spoon one-half of the oat batter into the prepared pan, sprinkle with the banana chips, and top with the remaining oat batter. Press down and level the top.

- Bake in a preheated oven, at 350°F, for 20–22 minutes, until golden.

- Remove from the oven and cut into 12 bars while still hot. Let cool in the pan.

 Baked Bananas with Passion Fruit and Honey Place 4 bananas in a preheated oven, at 425°F, or on a barbecue grill for 10 minutes, until charred. Meanwhile, scoop the pulp out of 4 passion fruit and mix with 1½ cups Greek yogurt and the finely grated zest of 1 orange. Split open the bananas, top with a large dollop of the passion fruit yogurt, and drizzle with 1 tablespoon honey.

 Chocolate and Honey-Baked Bananas Cut a slit in the skin of 4 bananas along one side. Stick 2 tablespoons chocolate disks into the cut and pour ½ tablespoon honey over the chocolate. Put each banana on a separate sheet of aluminum foil and seal to make a package. Place on a baking sheet and bake in a preheated oven, at 400°F, for 15–18 minutes, until the bananas are soft and the chocolate melted. Meanwhile, whisk 1¼ cups heavy cream with 2 tablespoons Cointreau and the finely grated zest of 1 orange. Serve the chocolate bananas with a dollop of the orange-flavored cream.

GLU-SWEE-VES

30 Lemon and Poppy Seed Muffins

Serves 4

2 tablespoons honey

2 tablespoons poppy seeds

juice of 2 lemons, plus the grated
zest of 1 lemon

1 stick unsalted butter, melted

½ cup granulated sugar

2 eggs

¾ cup plain yogurt

2¾ cups gluten-free flour blend

4 teaspoons gluten-free
baking powder

½ teaspoon baking soda

- Line a 12-section muffin pan with paper liners.

- Put the honey into a small saucepan over medium heat and add the poppy seeds, lemon zest, and one-half of the lemon juice. Heat until the honey is melted, then remove from the heat and pour into a bowl. Stir in the remaining lemon juice and let cool for 1–2 minutes.

- Whisk in the melted butter, sugar, eggs, and yogurt.

- Sift the flour, baking powder, and baking soda into a large bowl and pour in the yogurt mixture. Gently mix together until just combined; do not overmix.

- Divide among the paper muffin liners and bake in a preheated oven, at 375°F, for 15–18 minutes, until golden. Cool on a wire rack.

 Lemon and Poppy Seed Desserts

Mix together 1 cup lemon curd, 2 cups crème fraîche, 1 tablespoon poppy seeds, and the grated zest of 1 lemon. Stir in 6 crushed amaretti cookies and spoon into 4 glasses to serve.

 Lemon and Poppy Seed Scones

Sift 2 cups gluten-free flour blend into a bowl with 1 tablespoon gluten-free baking powder. Rub in 4 tablespoons unsalted butter until the mixture resembles fine bread crumbs. Stir in ¼ cup granulated sugar, the grated zest of 1 lemon, and 1 tablespoon poppy seeds. Whisk together 1 egg and ⅔ cup milk and pour into the flour mixture. Bring the dough together. Using an ice cream scoop, scoop 8–10 mounds of the dough onto a baking sheet. Bake in a preheated oven, at 425°F, for 12–15 minutes, until risen and golden. Serve warm with dollops of crème fraîche or Greek yogurt and lemon curd.

3⬤ Chocolate Orange Shortbread

Serves 4

1 stick unsalted butter, softened
¼ cup granulated sugar
grated zest of 1 orange
¼ cup unsweetened
  cocoa powder
⅓ cup gluten-free flour blend

- Line a baking sheet with parchment paper.

- Cream together the butter, sugar, and orange zest until light and fluffy.

- Mix in the cocoa powder and flour and bring together until you have a ball of dough. Cover and chill for 10 minutes.

- Shape the mixture into walnut-size balls and place on the baking sheet, making sure they are well spaced.

- Bake in a preheated oven, at 375°F, for 5 minutes. Remove the sheet from the oven and lightly press down each ball of dough with your finger. Return to the oven and bake for another 5–7 minutes, until the dough has started to crisp on top.

- Place on a wire rack to cool completely.

 Chocolate Brownie Orange Pudding
Place 8 oz chopped semisweet chocolate, ⅓ cup granulated sugar, and ½ cup heavy cream in a small saucepan over low heat. Pour in ¼ cup hot water and stir until the chocolate has melted and the sauce is hot. Pour the sauce over 4 prepared gluten-free brownies and serve with the segments of 2 oranges, a dollop of crème fraîche, and a sprinkling of unsweetened cocoa powder.

 Chocolate Orange Scones Sift 2 cups gluten-free flour blend into a bowl with 1 tablespoon gluten-free baking powder, the grated zest of 1 orange, and 1 tablespoon unsweetened cocoa powder. Rub in 4 tablespoons unsalted butter until the mixture resembles fine bread crumbs. Stir in ¼ cup granulated sugar. Whisk together 1 egg and ⅔ cup milk and pour into the flour mixture. Bring the dough together. Using an ice cream scoop, scoop 8–10 mounds of the dough onto a baking sheet. Bake in a preheated oven, at 425°F, for 12–15 minutes, until risen and golden. Serve warm with dollops of crème fraîche or Greek yogurt and grated chocolate.

30 Crispy Cornbread

Serves 4

1 tablespoon lard
1 tablespoon butter, melted
1 tablespoon vegetable oil
2 scallions, diced
1 red chile, seeded and diced
1 cup corn kernels
1 cup cornmeal
1½ tablespoons gluten-free
  flour blend
2 teaspoons gluten-free
  baking powder
1 teaspoon baking soda
pinch of salt
2 teaspoons superfine or
  granulated sugar
1 egg, beaten
¾ cup buttermilk

- Grease an 8 inch round cake pan with the lard and place in a preheated oven, at 400°F, to heat.

- Put the butter and oil in a skillet over medium heat, add the scallions, chile, and corn, and cook for 1 minute, then remove from the heat.

- In a large bowl, sift together the cornmeal, flour, baking powder, baking soda, salt, and sugar. Make a well in the center.

- Beat together the egg and buttermilk, then pour into the well and gradually bring the mixture together with a fork.

- Stir in the scallion mixture.

- Remove the cake pan from the oven and pour in the corn batter. Return to the oven and bake for 20–23 minutes, until golden.

- Cool on a wire rack and cut into wedges to serve.

Cornbread French Toast

Melt 4 tablespoons butter in a large skillet. Whisk together 3 eggs and ½ cup heavy cream and dip in 6 thick slices of cornbread. Add to the skillet and cook for 3–4 minutes on each side, until golden. Meanwhile, cook 12 slices unsmoked bacon under a preheated medium broiler until crisp. Top the French toast with the bacon and drizzle with maple syrup to serve.

Cornbread Muffins

Brush a 12-section muffin pan with 1 tablespoon melted butter. Slice the kernels off 1 large cob of corn. Melt 2 tablespoons butter in a saucepan over medium heat, add the corn, 1 small diced onion, and ½ seeded and diced red chile, and cook for 2–3 minutes. Sift together 1¼ cup gluten-free flour blend, 1 cup cornmeal, and 2 teaspoons gluten-free baking powder. Stir in ½ cup shredded cheddar cheese and a pinch of salt. Whisk together 2 eggs, 4 tablespoons butter, melted, 1¼ cups buttermilk, and ½ cup milk. Stir the wet ingredients into the dry with the corn mixture, then divide among the muffin cups. Bake in a preheated oven, at 375°F, for 18–20 minutes, until golden and cooked through.

30 Chocolate Raspberry Cake

Serves 6–8

oil, for greasing
8 eggs, separated
pinch of salt
12 oz semisweet chocolate
1¼ sticks unsalted butter
¼ cup granulated sugar
1 cup crème fraîche
grated zest of 1 orange
3 cups raspberries
confectioners' sugar, for dusting

- Grease two 7 inch round cake pans.

- Whisk the egg yolks with the salt.

- Melt the chocolate and butter in a heatproof bowl set over a saucepan of gently simmering water. Let the melted chocolate cool for 2–3 minutes, then fold in the egg yolks.

- In a grease-free bowl, whisk the egg whites until forming stiff peaks, then gradually whisk in the sugar.

- Fold the egg whites into the chocolate mixture and pour into the prepared pans. Bake in a preheated oven, at 350°F, for 15 minutes, then remove from the pans and let cool.

- Meanwhile, mix together the crème fraîche and orange zest.

- Spread the orange cream over one of the cakes and top with one-half of the raspberries. Place the other cake on top and decorate with the remaining raspberries. Dust with confectioners' sugar to serve.

 Chocolate Desserts with Raspberry Coulis Put 1 cup heavy cream and ⅓ cup sugar in a saucepan and bring to a boil, stirring a few times to melt the sugar. Put 8 oz chopped semisweet chocolate, 2 egg yolks, and the grated zest of 1 orange in a food processor. With the food processor running, pour in the hot cream and process until the chocolate melts. Spoon into 4 glasses and serve with a tablespoon of prepared raspberry coulis.

 Chocolate Cakes with Raspberry Preserves Sift together 2¾ cups gluten-free flour blend, ¼ teaspoon unsweetened cocoa powder, and 1 teaspoon gluten-free baking powder into a bowl. Rub in 1¼ sticks butter until the mixture resembles fine bread crumbs. Stir in ½ cup granulated sugar, ⅓ cup dried currants, ¼ cup chocolate chips, and the finely grated zest of 1 lemon, then make a well in the center. Whisk together 2 eggs, 2 teaspoons vegetable oil, and 2 teaspoons lemon juice, and beat into the flour mixture to make a thick batter. Put a lightly oiled skillet over medium heat and spoon in mounds of 2–3 teaspoons of the batter, pressing them down lightly to make cakes. Cook for 2–3 minutes on each side, until lightly golden. Serve spread with raspberry preserves and a dollop of crème fraîche or whipped cream.

10 Lemon and Turkish Delight Syllabub

Serves 4

2 tablespoons rose water

¼ cup superfine sugar

1¾ cup heavy cream

2 tablespoons lemon juice

3½ oz Turkish Delight, diced

grated zest of 1 lemon

- Put the rose water into a large bowl and stir in the sugar until it dissolves.

- Add the cream and whip until soft peaks form. Stir in the lemon juice and Turkish Delight and divide among 4 glasses to serve.

- Serve sprinkled with the lemon zest.

 2 Molten Chocolate Cakes with Turkish Delight Syllabub Melt 1 stick unsalted butter with 4 oz semisweet chocolate in a heatproof bowl set over a saucepan of gently simmering water. Whisk together 2 eggs, 2 egg yolks, and ⅔ cup superfine sugar until pale and fluffy. Gently fold in the chocolate mixture, then fold in 2 tablespoons gluten-free flour blend. Spoon into 4 lightly oiled and cocoa-dusted molds and bake in a preheated oven, at 400°F, for 12 minutes. Meanwhile, whisk ⅔ cup heavy cream with 2 tablespoons superfine or granulated sugar until soft peaks form, then fold in the zest and juice of ½ lemon and 2 oz diced Turkish Delight. Chill. Turn out the cakes and serve with the syllabub.

 3 Meringue Roulade with Lemon Syllabub and Turkish Delight Filling Whisk 4 egg whites until stiff, then whisk in 1 cup superfine sugar, a tablespoon at a time, until the mixture is thick and glossy. Grease an 8 x 12 inch jellyroll pan, line it with parchment paper, and sprinkle with ⅔ cup dry shredded coconut. Bake in a preheated oven, at 400°F, for 15–18 minutes, until just firm to the touch. Turn out onto a piece of parchment paper, then remove the backing paper and loosely roll, using the parchment paper underneath. Let cool for 5 minutes. Mix together the rind and juice of 2 lemons and ¼ cup honey, stirring until the honey has dissolved. Pour in 2½ cups heavy cream and whisk until soft. Unroll the meringue, spread with the cream, and sprinkle with 2 oz diced Turkish Delight. Gently reroll to serve.

30 Coconut and Golden Raisin Cookies

Serves 4

1 stick unsalted butter, plus
    extra for greasing
2 tablespoons light corn syrup
1 egg, beaten
1¼ cups dry shredded coconut
⅓ cup rice flour
1 teaspoon gluten-free
    baking powder
2 cup firmly packed dark
    brown sugar
2 cups golden raisins

- Lightly grease 2 baking sheets.

- In a small saucepan, melt together the corn syrup and butter. Let cool for 3–4 minutes, then beat in the egg.

- Put the remaining ingredients into a large bowl, pour in the syrup mixture, and mix well.

- Place teaspoons of the dough onto the prepared baking sheets (the dough should yield 12), allowing space for the cookies to spread. Bake in a preheated oven, at 350°F, for 10–15 minutes, until golden. Let cool on a wire rack.

 1 Coconut and Golden Raisin Desserts Toast 2 tablespoons dry shredded coconut under a preheated medium broiler for 3–4 minutes, until golden. Stir 2 tablespoons dry shredded coconut into 1½ cups Greek yogurt, then stir in 2 teaspoons honey. Spoon one-half of this mixture into 4 glasses. Top with 1 tablespoon golden raisins, 1 peeled, pitted, and diced mango, and ½ cup raspberries, then spoon over the remaining yogurt. Sprinkle with the toasted coconut and drizzle with a little more honey to serve.

 2 Coconut and Golden Raisin Scones Sift 2 cups gluten-free flour blend into a bowl with 1 tablespoon gluten-free baking powder. Stir in 1 tablespoon dry shredded coconut. Rub in 4 tablespoons unsalted butter until the mixture resembles fine bread crumbs. Stir in ¼ cup granulated sugar and ⅓ cup golden raisins. Whisk together 1 egg and ⅔ cup milk and pour into the flour mixture. Bring the dough together. Using an ice cream scoop, scoop 8–10 mounds of the dough onto a baking sheet. Bake in a preheated oven, at 425°F, for 12–15 minutes, until risen and golden.

3⦿ Lemon and Raspberry Cheesecake Tartlets

Serves 4

1½ cups walnuts
4 dates, pitted
2 tablespoons maple syrup
4 (3 inch) store-bought individual pie shells
¾ cup mascarpone cheese
grated zest and juice of 1 lemon
2 tablespoons confectioners' sugar
1 cup raspberries

- Put the walnuts into a bowl, cover with cold water, and let stand for 10 minutes. Drain.

- Put the walnuts, dates, and maple syrup into a food processor and blend until they all come together. Divide the mixture among the pastry shells and press into the bottom and sides. Chill.

- Meanwhile, mix together the mascarpone, lemon zest, lemon juice, and confectioners' sugar. Divide the mixture among the pastry shells. Chill.

- Meanwhile, make a raspberry coulis by pressing the raspberries through a strainer to remove the seeds.

- Remove the tartlets from their pans and place each one on a small plate, then top with a drizzle of raspberry coulis.

 Lemon and Raspberry Soda Floats Divide 8 scoops (1 quart) vanilla ice cream among 4 tall glasses. Pour in enough lemonade to fill the glass. Add 3–4 raspberries to each glass, sprinkle with the grated zest of 1 lemon, and serve with long spoons.

 Lemon Soufflés with Raspberry Coulis Mix 1 tablespoon cornstarch with a little water, then put into a food processor with 2 chopped bananas, the grated zest of 2 lemons, and 1 tablespoon lemon juice and process until nearly smooth. In a grease-free bowl, whisk 6 egg whites, gradually adding ¾ cup superfine sugar and 2 teaspoons lemon juice, until smooth soft peaks form. Put the banana mixture into a large bowl and gently fold in the meringue, then divide the mixture among 4 buttered and sugared ramekins. Level the top of each one and make sure the edges are clean. Bake in a preheated oven, at 375°F, for 10–12 minutes, until risen and golden. Meanwhile, make a raspberry coulis as above and spoon over the soufflés to serve.

Index

Page references in *italics*
indicate photographs

Acknowledgments

Recipes by Joy Skipper
Executive Editor Eleanor Maxfield
Editors Katy Denny and Alex Stetter
Art Direction Tracy Killick and Geoff Fennell for Tracy Killick Art Direction and Design
Original design concept www.gradedesign.com
Designer Tracy Killick for Tracy Killick Art Direction and Design
Photographer William Shaw
Prop Stylist Liz Hippisley
Senior Production Manager Katherine Hockley